Andreas Dripke, Hang Nguyen, Jamal Qaiser

When China and Russia join forces...

The Challenge for the Free World

Andreas Dripke, Hang Nguyen, Jamal Qaiser

When China and Russia join forces...

The Challenge for the Free World

Diplomatic Council Publishing

1st Edition 2022

Bibliographic information of the German National Library:

The German National Library lists this publication in the Deutsche Nationalbibliografie;
detailed bibliographic data is available on the Internet at http://dnb.d-nb.de

Printed in the Federal Republic of Germany.

Design, cover and typesetting: IMS International Media Services, Wiesbaden

Translator: Maria Schmitz

Printed on acid-free paper.

Print ISBN: 978-3-98674-022-1

E-book ISBN: 978-3-98674-023-8

Dedicated to the next generation

This work is dedicated to our children, nephews and nieces.

They all represent the next generation. May they grow up in peace and freedom and, as adults, ensure that successive generations can also thrive in peace and freedom.

Andreas Dripke, Hang Nguyen, Jamal Qaiser

Contents

Preface

For many years, the narrative has developed in Germany and other European countries that the attitude of Russia and China towards each other is more or less friendly. At the same time, the impression had been created that the United States of America was the aggressor that Europe had to beware of.

The Cold War, the confrontation between the West and the Eastern bloc had long ceased. After the atrocities of World War I and World War II, a Third World War seemed to be out of the question. When the media spoke of "war" in recent years, the reference has been merely to an "economic war" or a "technology war".

Russia's invasion of Ukraine in February 2022 made it clear that all these "minor wars" over economics and technology harbour the danger of a real war.

With reference to American power play and the inadequacies of U.S. policy, it appeared over the years that Europe could adopt a neutral, virtually equal stance between the United States and Russia, on the one hand, and, above all, China on the other. In the highest European government circles, the idea of an independent European army was advanced in order to no longer have to play the role of junior partner in NATO, the intergovernmental military alliance.

The Russian invasion of Ukraine on 24 February 2022 has made all these considerations absurd. Without the economic, technological and, above all, military support of the United States of America, Europe would be lost. One may lament this but to ignore it would be fatal in the truest sense of the word, as the Ukrainian people have tragically experienced.

One must be clear that both the Soviet Union, of which "only" Russia is left at the moment, and the People's Republic of China share a fundamentally different view of humanity than the free West. The "old struggle" between capitalism and communism is by no means over, as it appeared to be after the end of the Cold War between the West and the Eastern bloc. It had only disappeared from the headlines but in the background the superpower arms race has continued unabated.

Let us take a count and assess the significance of this: There are three superpowers, namely the United States of America, Russia as the core of the former and gradually re-emerging Soviet Union, and the People's Republic of China. Two of them, Russia and China, are clearly committed to communism. The only capitalist superpower is the USA. It is illusory to believe that, in the face of these power dynamics, Europe can adopt a neutral position, reap the benefits of capitalism, and at the same time be "good friends" with communism.

One may lament the excesses of capitalism – and there are undoubtedly very many. But to conclude from this that life would be better in the communist paradigm has always been and remains a fallacy.

Germany should know better: The country was divided into a capitalist West and a communist East for 40 years. The East, then known as the German Democratic Republic, was fenced off by the GDR government to prevent people from fleeing in droves. There is no clearer image to document the lack of freedom under communism than that of encaging people like animals.

This is at least one, if not *the* decisive difference between capitalism and communism: freedom! Capitalism presupposes the freedom of the individual as a conception of humanity. This includes the freedom to make something of one's life, to find happiness but lamentably also the freedom to "screw up" one's life, to put it casually, to perish in misery. But to conclude from this that the state can – as is the premise of communism – enforce people's happiness to help all people to a state-guaranteed good life, is inhumane.

A political regime that has to draw an actual or even an invisible fence around "its" population to prevent people from fleeing in droves is per se unjust. A state whose government monitors and reprimands "its" citizens to the utmost in respect of their loyalty to the state, without subjecting itself to independent jurisdiction, cannot claim to be a constitutional state.

If we look at the global balance of power from this perspective, there is only one constitutional superpower, and that is the USA. There are undoubtedly many and good reasons to criticise the United States of America. But the alternatives – Russia, as the core of the former Soviet Union, and the People's Republic of China – are not viable options – at least not if the freedom of the individual and the rule of law of a society as an expression of justice are taken as standards.

For this reason, joint or even concerted action by the two communist superpowers China and Russia – a Sino-Soviet axis – is arguably the greatest threat to the free West, i.e. North America and Europe in particular. In this situation, it would be literally fatal for Europe to believe that it can adopt a mutual, virtually equal stance between all parties. In this camp formation, which is deplorable but hardly subject to change, Germany and Europe clearly belong to the Western camp.

However, even if there is unity, it is by no means certain that the West will be able to win an escalating conflict against the two communist superpowers. The People's Republic of China and Russia may not be "bosom friends", nor are Europe and the USA but they adhere to a similar ideology and the danger of a bloc formation is tangible. Should the Sino-Soviet cartel emerge, the West would have a tough time. It would be helpful if Europe took a clear stance in this situation.

Andreas Dripke, Hang Nguyen, Jamal Qaiser

First and Second World Wars

Wars have existed since time immemorial. But never have so many people died in such a brief time as in World War I and World War II. It is not least a terrifying prospect that in a Third World War even more people would lose their lives in an even shorter period, which is what drives peace activists as well as responsible politicians all over the world to try to prevent a third recurrence.

The high death tolls

Almost 20 million people lost their lives in the First World War, including around 9.7 million soldiers and around 10 million civilians. The losses came from many countries: Australia (61,900 dead), Belgium (104,900), Bulgaria (187,500), the German Empire (2.46 million), Denmark (720), Canada (66,900), the Republic of France (1.697 million), Kingdom of Greece (176,000), United Kingdom (994,100), British India (74,000), the Kingdom of Italy (1.24 million), Japan (415), Montenegro (3,000), Austria-Hungary (1.567 million), Ottoman Empire (5 million), New Zealand (18,000), Newfoundland (1,200), Norway (1890), Portugal (89,200 Kingdom of Romania (680,000), Russian Empire (3.311 million), Kingdom of Serbia (725,000), Sweden (870), South African Union (9,400), United States of America (117,400). In addition, an estimated 21 million people were injured as a result of the war.[1]

In World War II everything got much worse. The fighting began, apart from a few skirmishes on the German-Polish border, on 1 September 1939, when the liner "Schleswig-Holstein" opened fire on the Westerplatte near Danzig, and ended on 8 May 1945 at 11:01 p m. That is 2077 days or 49,842 hours and 16 minutes. During this time, around 1,000 people died every hour. Overall, World War II claimed the lives of approximately 50 million people, including 39 million civilians. Other estimates even assume around 60 to 80 million deaths in World War II.[2]

The victims came from numerous countries: Australia (30,000 deaths), Belgium (60,000), Bulgaria (32,000), China (13.5 million), Germany (6.355 million), Finland (91,700), France (360,000), Greece (180,000), the United Kingdom (332, 825), India (3.024 million), Italy (300,000), Japan (3.76 million), Yugoslavia (1.69 million), Canada (43,190), New Zealand (10,000), Netherlands (220,000), Norway (10,000), South Africa (9,000), Philippines (100,000), Poland (6 million), Romania (378,000), Soviet Union (27 million), Czechoslovakia (90,000), Hungary (950,000), USA (407,316).[3]

Well over 100 million dead and injured in two world wars within around 30 years. Soldiers, civilians, men, women, children, destroyed lives, extinguished hopes, indescribable horrors, infinite suffering – in the face of this gigantic destructiveness, the international community wanted to do everything possible with a "global peace organisation" to prevent or at least contain further killing. After the First World War with 20 million losses, the international community founded the League of Nations with a single goal: to prevent the Second World War. Unfortunately, the

League of Nations failed. Around 20 years later, preparations began for the Second World War, which cost over 50 million lives.[4]

The United Nations Organisation was established to prevent a Third World War. [5]

Has it succeeded so far? Yes, as far as no one has yet declared World War III. No, as far as more wars are raging in the world today than ever before. The global number of military conflicts has been rising steadily for years, as has the number of victims and refugees who want to escape the wars and save their lives.[6] Russia's invasion of Ukraine on 24 February 2022 has highlighted how close warfare has come to Europe. But long before that, wars raged almost around the globe.

Innumerable wars

The counts by the Heidelberg Institute for International Conflict Research showed an average of 18 wars between 2011 and 2019 that took place around the globe every year.[7] Thereby, the Institute referred only to "real wars", not to mere military confrontations or conflicts in which violence is occasionally deployed. The institute counted 21 wars in 2020, 15 in 2019, 16 in 2018, 20 in 2017, 18 in 2016, 19 in 2015, 21 in 2014, 18 in 2012 and 20 in 2011. Before 2011, the situation looked much better. In 2010 there were "only" six wars, in the year before that there were "only" seven wars. In addition to these "real wars", the Heidelberg Institute also recorded so-called "limited wars", which should be added to the "real" ones. Here the numbers were similarly high: 19 limited wars in 2020, 23 in 2019, 25 in 2018, 20 in 2017 and 2016, 24 in 2015, 25 in 2013 and 2012, 18 in 2011, 22 in 2010 and 24 in 2009. An order of magnitude higher by a factor of ten is obtained if one also considers conflicts in the world. The Heidelberg Institute named 319 conflicts in 2020, of which more than half – 180 – were classified as violent.[8]

The figures were similarly high in previous years: 385 conflicts in 2019, of which 196 were violent, 374 conflicts in 2018, of which 214 were violent, 385 conflicts in 2017, of which 222 were violent, 402 conflicts in 2016, of which 226 were violent, 409 conflicts in 2015, of these again 223 were violent, 424 conflicts in 2014, of which 223 were violent, 414 conflicts in 2014, of which 221 were violent.

Was it better in the past? The analyses by the Heidelberg Institute for International Conflict Research say "yes". In 1992, the first year the institute started its research series, the report at the time showed over 100 conflicts and five wars. In 1993 there were already 119 conflicts and 23 wars. Without presenting the Institute's methodology in detail here or discussing the question of defining the differences between "real wars", "limited wars" and "violent conflicts" in detail, one thing is certain: violence is increasing worldwide, not decreasing. People are uprooted, injured, killed. Every day 500 people are killed on average in violent conflicts, i.e. 182,000 war deaths per annum. Together that is well over 12 million deaths since the end of World War II.[9]

These numbers could even be too conservative. A study by Global Research suggests that at least 20 million people in 37 states have died in combat operations that can be traced back directly to the United States since the end of World War II. The countries were either attacked directly or driven into civil wars by US intelligence activities.[10]

All these figures are based on estimates, are subject to questions of definition and are often politically motivated. The crucial question in relation to the subject of this book is, however, simple: Will a clash between the two communist powers, China and Russia, on the one hand, and the Western camp, on the other, lead to another "really big war", a world war?

"Everyone knows WW III will be a nuclear war"

One may rightly complain about the multitude of conflicts around the globe but how much greater would the suffering wrought by a Third World War be in which nuclear weapons were used? In the Cold War between the Western nations under the leadership of the USA and the Eastern Bloc of the Soviet Union under the leadership of Russia, a nuclear conflict was successfully averted.

But there is no guarantee that in the present-day conflict between China, Russia and the United States, for example, it will again be possible to avert a battle with nuclear weapons. In the wake of the Russian invasion of Ukraine in the spring of 2022, both a "nuclear war" and a "Third World War" were in the offing – or more precisely, both terms were used.

Russian Foreign Minister Sergei Lavrov stated bluntly: "Everyone knows that a Third World War will be a nuclear war. This question, however, is only a concern of Western politicians and not of the Russians.[11] In fact, Russian President Vladimir Putin shocked the world by announcing that his country's nuclear strike forces would be alerted.[12] China, on the other hand, has no interest whatsoever in a global armed conflict. Not because the

People's Republic is inspired by peace but simply because China is not yet prepared to face a full-scale military confrontation with the USA in the foreseeable future. That is why China has (for the time being) shifted the rivalry to other areas such as the economy and technology.

In this constellation, it is important to find an answer to the question of where Europe stands in the struggle between the three superpowers and what role Europe can play in it.

The culture war

Occasionally, the perception is that Europe is on the fence – the USA on the one side, China – and since February 2022 – also Russia on the other. Those who talk like this completely fail to realise that our German and European societies, despite all their differences, have much more in common with the United States of America than with their Chinese or Russian counterparts when it comes to their conception of the state and society. But this is by no means a general finding among the German population.

In the dispute between China and the USA, Germany seems to have maintained equal relations with both countries, at least since the coronavirus outbreak in the early 2020s. In a survey conducted at the height of the 2020 crisis, the German population was divided on the question of whether close relations with the USA or with China are more important for Germany. Asked about this, 37 per cent named the USA and 36 per cent China. Another 13 per cent bet on both countries. Only one year earlier, one in two Germans (50 per cent) had spoken out in favour of a close relationship with the USA. Just under one in four (24 per cent) had given preference to China.[13] In view of this development, more than 75 years after the end of the Second World War, one surely could speak of a realignment in the geopolitical power structure in the 2020s.

Since 2021, US President Joe Biden has been trying to counter Europe's slide out of the US sphere of influence. In the first year of his term and the last year of German Chancellor Angela Merkel's term, both sides signed a "Washington Declaration" that underlines the shared values of both countries. In addition, a "German-American Future Forum" and an "Economic Dialogue" were agreed upon and a "Climate and Energy Partnership" was signed – including a general commitment to the struggle against climate change.[14] However, Germany and the USA were less concerned with the global climate than with the bilateral political climate. Biden is determined to form a political bloc of free and democratic states under global US leadership against the communist power structures in China and Russia. The Russian war of aggression against Ukraine since February 2022 was convenient for the US president in that it virtually drove Europe into the arms of the USA. The question of the significance of NATO, for example, took a back seat in the face of the Russian invasion of Ukraine.

Karl Marx is Chinese and Russian

It should not be overlooked that China, in its ascent, is by no means embracing capitalism but remains committed to the ideals of Karl Marx. The current state capitalism is only understood as a preliminary stage to socialism. Under Mikhail Gorbachev, the Soviet Union of the time had introduced liberal, free-market and almost democratic elements into the Russian state system with "glasnost" (openness) and "perestroika" (restructuring). It was not in the national interest: The Soviet Union disintegrated, leaving no remnants of the former Eastern Bloc. China has learned from this development.

On 1 July 2021, the Communist Party (CP) of China celebrated its centenary. with great pomp. The CP is the only decisive political force in the world's most populous country. With about 95 million members, it is also the second largest political party in the world – only India's Bharatiya Janata Party has more. Moreover, China's CP is the last and most long-lived world-scale communist party. By comparison, the Communist Party of the Russian Federation does not even have 200,000 members.[15] After the collapse of the Soviet Union, the Russian Soviet Socialist Federative Republic (RSFSR) had been renamed the Russian Federation on 25 December 1991.[16] In this book, the term Russia is predominantly used in this regard.

Historians argue about the question of why communism survived in China, unlike in the Soviet Union, for example. One plausible explanation is that in China, communist ideology has proven to be particularly flexible. CP co-founder Mao Zedong, as well as his most influential successors Deng Xiaoping and Xi Jinping in the office of party leader, added new elements to Marxist-Leninist ideology and turned it into an instrument of absolutist-style political control.[17]

In the propaganda narrative, the history of contemporary China is intrinsically associated with the history of the Party. In its name, Mao Zedong initiated the industrialisation of the country. Millions died in waves of purges in the 1950s, during the so-called Great Leap Forward and the Cultural Revolution. Deng Xiaoping, as an absolutist ruler, liberalised the Chinese economy and suppressed the democracy movements with bloodshed.[18] The incumbent Xi Jinping is now apparently determined to challenge the global supremacy of the USA and place China first among the superpowers. He has the time to do so until 2049: In March 2018, the Chinese People's Congress lifted term limits for the president.[19] While Vladimir Putin can still rule until 2036 according to the Russian constitution, his colleague from the People's Republic of China can be head of state until the end of his life. And until then he obviously still has a lot to do.[20]

Global competition between social systems

China wants to become the world's strongest economic power even before 2050. At the latest when this goal is achieved, will the global competition of social systems arise: The Western liberal capitalism of Europe and North America will then, at the latest, probably have to brace itself for an attack by the Marxist-socialist model. From the Chinese perspective, socialism is better suited to provide wealth for most of the population than capitalism, which from this perspective only provides wealth for a fraction of the people. The Silk Road project thus certainly also harbours the political motivation to successively establish this model throughout Asia, Europe and Africa. The widening chasm between Europe and the USA over the years thus suits Chinese policy very well. The US position "America first" is opposed by the counter-model "China only", while Europe is more likely to fall into small-scale nationalisation. The Russian invasion of Ukraine in 2022, meanwhile, has strengthened the ties between Europe and the USA like no event before. It was virtually a wake-up call to the Western world not to underestimate the two communist power blocs as opponents. US President Joe Biden, who took office in 2021, has already made it clear that his country will not stand idly by and watch the rise of either China or Russia.[21]

The US will fiercely oppose especially China's goal of global innovation leadership. This means that the conflict with Europe is pre-programmed: In future, China will try even harder to take over companies in Europe that are particularly strong in know-how and technology. In fact, this process has long been underway. After the former US President Donald Trump accused China of unfair trade practices and denounced the large deficit in the exchange of goods between the two countries, China in return accused the US of "trade tyranny". Former German Chancellor Gerhard Schröder has long since identified Europe's place in this conflict and suggested that, far from being set up as part of an American trade conflict with China, Europe should seize the opportunity and side with China. "We cannot put up with being treated like an occupied country," said Gerhard Schröder, referring to the behaviour of the USA.[22] It would be a departure from transatlantic friendship towards a Eurasian bridge. US President Joe Biden has been trying to counteract this rapprochement between Europe and China since 2021. He wants to forge a global alliance against China's supremacy – and to this end he apparently wants to turn the G7 countries (Germany, France, Great Britain, Italy, Japan, Canada and the United States) into an anti-China alliance. In essence, Biden calls on the international community to choose between China and the USA (in favour of the USA, of course), i.e. not to take a middle path or adopt a more or less neutral role. With regard to Russia, the question of any close ties has been resolved after the military invasion of Ukraine.

Europe looks out primarily for itself

However, Europe is a continent that looks out primarily for itself. European society has hardly any vision for the future of its own continent, let alone the world. European politics largely takes its cue from this lack of imagination on the part of society, the sole aim of which is to preserve today's prosperity and continue to bask in complacency. Increasingly more people in Europe, nevertheless, are beginning to suspect that this complacency and lack of vision will lead to Europe's decline. Local politicians hardly think five years ahead. Chinese politicians propose and dispose in time frames of 50 years and longer.

The best example of this is the development of a Eurasian railway network, which China is driving forward. With an investment of over 130 billion dollars, China is building a high-speed rail network between Asia and Europe. The aim is to transport goods from China to Europe within one day. In the 2020s, China wants to transport millions of containers by this overland route. Since 2020, the railways have been bringing ready-to-run cars – not just components – from China to Europe.

On 13 July 2021, the first goods train arrived in Wilhelmshaven on the new direct connection between the Chinese province of Anhui and the JadeWeserPort. The train with 100 containers had started in China on 25 June and travelled via Kazakhstan, Russia and Poland to Germany.[23] Soon there will be regular rail services between China and the port.

The primary danger that China sees in Russia's military posturing is that the land connections between the People's Republic and Europe will suffer. For a stable railway network as a basis for reliable Sino-European coordination, the overland routes through Russia and partly also Ukraine play an essential role. The Chinese regime therefore does not by any means savour the warlike unrest that Russia has been bringing to its neighbouring states even before 2022.

It can therefore be assumed that China will, as it did in 2022 in the fight over Ukraine, exert a soothing influence on Russia in order to prevent the conflict from escalating too far. Wherever Moscow succeeds in restraining the influence of the USA, China is certainly happy with Russia's activities -- but not if a "major war" is launched (prematurely). For the Chinese want to exploit the next few years primarily for further economic and political networking around the globe.

China and the APEC-states

In its counter-positioning to the USA, China is trying to bind as much of the world to itself as possible. The countries of the Asia-Pacific Economic Cooperation (APEC) play a key role in this. The 21 APEC countries represent about 2.8 billion people and a good half of the world's economic output. At the 2018 APEC Summit in Port Moresby, China's leader Xi took two days to hold a special summit with eight small Pacific states that play an extremely significant role in the region. For it is precisely there, on groups of islands that US troops had partly wrested from Japanese occupation in the Second World War, that China has been building new infrastructures of immense strategic importance for some time.

The approach is as simple as it is effective: Beijing provides the predominantly weak governments with donations and loans in order to create economic and ultimately political dependencies. The model works not only in the Pacific but from Southeast Asia to Africa and increasingly in Europe, as the success of the New Silk Road shows.

Washington regards this development with mistrust. As US Vice President Mike Pence said at the 2018 APEC Summit: "Our nation's security and prosperity depend on this vital region, and the United States will continue to ensure that all nations, large and small, can thrive and prosper in a free and open Indo-Pacific". The use of the term "Indo-Pacific" instead of "Pacific" is no accident: US strategists want to make it clear that America's orientation extends beyond the Strait of Malacca to India. Together with Australia and Japan, India and the United States form the loose association of the "Quad" (Quadrilateral Security Dialogue). The four countries agree on one thing above all: they harbour a deep mistrust of China.

At the same time, the US has launched a diplomatic charm offensive in all countries uncomfortable with China's growing supremacy. These include Vietnam and Malaysia but also the island republic of Taiwan, which Beijing regards as a renegade province, and which is supplied with weapons by the Pentagon. Moreover, the US launched a $60 billion financial programme to help strategically important countries. A new federal agency for US investments in developing countries was created specifically for this purpose. The 60 billion US dollars allocated for this were of course ridiculous in view of the Chinese trillions for the New Silk Road. But at least it was a symbolic act to show that US allies do not have to go away empty-handed. Whether it will be enough is doubtful.

Of all people, Rodrigo Duterte, the president of the Philippines, arguably the closest US ally in the Pacific, said at the 2018 APEC

Summit, which the US president himself did not attend but only sent Vice President Mike Pence: "China is there. That's a reality and America and everybody else should realize that they are there".

This is not only the attitude of the Philippines. South Korean President Moon Jae-In has long maintained close ties with China because he knows that Korean reunification will never be possible without Chinese consent – all the more or less doltish negotiations of then US President Donald Trump with North Korea were to no avail.

Japan pursued a two-fold strategy. After Trump's inauguration in 2017, Japan's Prime Minister Shinzo Abe was the first head of government on the spot to personally congratulate the newly elected US President. But in October 2018, he travelled to Beijing with a delegation of more than 1,000 companies to promote Sino-Japanese economic relations.

All these countries in the Pacific had flourished under the auspices of US supremacy after World War II: besides Japan, the arch enemy from World War II, also Malaysia, Singapore, South Korea, Taiwan, Thailand and even communist Vietnam, the pawn of the Cold War. But in the face of China's unstoppable ascent, the balance of power in the region is shifting: the US is no longer the undisputed ruler.

Competition for the world order

In 2017, the then newly elected US President Donald Trump made his first state visit to China. Trump raved about Xi Jinping as a "great friend" and spoke of the "great chemistry" between him and the Chinese leader. Not even proxy wars were in sight at the time, apart from ongoing skirmishes at sea.

But just a few weeks after Trump's return from Beijing in 2017, the US administration gave the National Security Strategy an update and clearly defined the US-China relationship as a "contest between those who favour repressive systems and those who favour free societies". Shortly afterwards, the US Department of Defence followed up with an updated National Defence Strategy, in which China was classified as a "strategic competitor" to the US, ahead of Russia. The Pentagon described China as a "revisionist power" that undermines the "economic, diplomatic and security decisions" of the US.

In less than no time, the matter escalated into mutual suspicions and accusations. The FBI Director Christopher Wray, who was in office at the time, attested to China being "the broadest, most complicated, most long-term counterintelligence threat" to the USA. The former arch-enemy Russia was concerned with remaining "relevant" after the fall of the Soviet Union but "China is fighting tomorrow's battle". The comparison with Moscow is significant; for a long time, the United States of America assumed that it would ultimately be able to bring China to its knees just as it did Russia. At his first press conference in office in March 2021, US President Joe Biden referred to China saying "I see stiff competition".[24]

But the Chinese government is obviously just as determined to stand up to US pressure, at whatever level and of whatever kind. The Beijing newspaper Global Times expressed the state's raison d'être clearly in 2021 saying China was a great and powerful nation, and whether the confrontation turned out to be economic or military, the price would be daunting.[25]

Respect for human rights is seen as a central conflict between the USA and its Western allies, on the one hand, and communist China – and of course Russia – on the other.

Universal Declaration of Human Rights

On 10 December 1948 at three o'clock in the night, Eleanor Roosevelt, chair of the United Nations Commission on Human Rights, proudly proclaimed the "Universal Declaration of Human Rights". For the very first time in human history, rights were formulated to apply to all people regardless of age, gender, nationality or race. The Declaration was to be the "common ideal to be reached by all peoples and nations". It has since been translated into more than 200 languages.[26]

Prior to this, eight people from Australia, Chile, China, France, Lebanon, the Soviet Union, Great Britain and the United States had worked on the Declaration for two years. Without any dissenting votes and with eight abstentions, the then 58 member states of the United Nations adopted the "Universal Declaration of Human Rights" in the Palais de Chaillot in Paris. Some of the human rights proclaimed in the Declaration are the right to life, liberty and security, the prohibition of slavery and torture, freedom of thought and belief, freedom of expression, education, work, health and well-being.

These tenets are undoubtedly a milestone for humanity but when it comes to upholding human rights, the United Nations has often seemed helpless. In the "tripartite war" between the

United States, China and Russia, the UN does not play a laudable role – and there is nothing to suggest that this could change in the future if the conflicts escalate.

The United Nations is not succeeding in preventing large-scale genocides, neither in Africa nor in Asia. Whether in Rwanda, Myanmar or other regions of the world, the power of the United Nations to enforce human rights has always and repeatedly been infinitesimal. In many cases, there was hardly any will to do so.

"We are at a nadir. Human rights do not count for anything anymore," was the expressed resignation of Carla Del Ponte, Chief Prosecutor of the International Criminal Court in The Hague from 1999 to 2007, and in this capacity responsible for dealing with war crimes in the former Yugoslavia and Rwanda. She delivered a damning verdict on the UN Human Rights Council in Geneva: half of the 47 countries that hold one of the rotating memberships violate human rights on a daily basis. Countries like China, Saudi Arabia and Burundi would therefore have to be expelled from the Council immediately. In 2017, she therefore resigned as Special Investigator of a UN Human Rights Council Commission of Inquiry into war crimes in Syria – because of the Commission's inaction.[27]

China and the EU under fire

Whenever the West accuses China of serious human rights violations, the Chinese side never tires of emphasising that the United Nations also regularly exposes alleged violations of human rights in the European Union and its member states. One example of this was the interference of David Kaye, UN Special

Rapporteur in the Protection of human rights, in the European copyright reform in spring 2019. Article 13 of this reform is incompatible with international principles of freedom of expression, Kaye found, and called on the European Parliament to discuss the outstanding issues with civil rights groups, artists, journalists and other representatives of civil society.[28]

But it is not only the EU that has to tolerate scrutiny by the UN as to whether it really does respect human rights. Individual member states are also under permanent scrutiny by the UN. For example, in the spring of 2019, the United Nations Economic and Social Council certified serious deficits in the implementation of social human rights by the Federal Republic of Germany. Countless older people lived "in degrading conditions" and did not receive "adequate care in certain nursing homes due to the lack of qualified staff". In 2019, the German government was asked, as it had been by the same UN body five years earlier, to provide more money for the training of healthcare workers as well as to inspect nursing homes "more frequently and thoroughly".

Furthermore, the UN criticised the German Hartz IV system ("Fourth Law for Modern Services in the Labour Market"). Almost 20 per cent of children in Germany live in poverty and it must be made easier for parents to receive social benefits. The UN demanded an increase in the basic income support in Germany and a stop to benefit cuts in case of violations of obligations by Hartz IV recipients. Furthermore, a higher minimum wage was demanded.[29] The UN also criticised the insecurity of medical care in Germany.

There is certainly some truth in all these criticisms and it would behove federal policy to address them. But these constant reminders from the UN naturally give China every opportunity to point out that the slate of Western states is by no means so clean in terms of human rights as to justify a moral high ground – or even the right to publicly criticise China in this matter. Moreover, China refers historically to colonisation, human trafficking and the Holocaust when it comes to human rights, in order to admonish Europeans and Americans to search their own consciences instead of criticising the People's Republic.[30] Russia's Vladimir Putin has also made it clear time and again over the years that his country does not want to play the "bogeyman". With largely fictitious accusations of anti-Russian and US-directed actions, as in Ukraine, or under the guise of fighting terrorism, as in Syria, Putin repeatedly justifies his cruel actions by claiming that he wants to protect threatened minorities.

The dispute between the Western states on the one hand and China and Russia on the other is not so much about human rights as some European or US politicians would have us believe. Rather, the focus is on geopolitical supremacy.

We seem to be heading again towards a world divided into two competing blocs, a Western bloc led by the US with Europe as a junior partner, and a Eurasian bloc with (a lot of) China and (some of) Russia. In other words, the United States of America and the People's Republic of China – the epitome of capitalism and communism respectively – are vying for world supremacy, while Europe and Russia join forces with the superpower most affiliated to them, respectively.

Global power centres

Interstate conflicts are older than the concept of nation states – in the past they were tribal feuds, religious obsessions or power struggles between dynasties. From these often-bloody conflicts, the idea of peaceful cooperation has developed over several centuries to settle conflicts peacefully before they lead to war. Today, we speak of "international institutions" in which states seek solutions to contentious issues that are acceptable to all. For a long time, multilateralism, i.e. cooperation within an international community – going beyond bilateralism between just two countries – was considered the way to a peaceful world. The United Nations Organisation (UNO) stands for this global multilateral approach like no other world organisation.

The so-called international institutions also play a role in the dispute between China, Russia and the United States– but only a minor role, by no means the main one. Events after the Second World War have shown that the United States as well as China and Russia accept the UN as a pawn for their own intrigues rather than as a moral or even power-political authority.

Anyone who wants to understand today's confrontation between the two superpowers and Russia's aspiration to rejoin the ranks must be aware of the events that occurred at the United Nations after the end of the Second World War and consider the decline of multilateralism since 2015.

International law

The idea of a community of states is not new. The term "international law" was first mentioned in 1625 in the book "On the law of war and peace" by the Dutch legal scholar Hugo Grotius. In 1795, the philosopher Immanuel Kant advanced the idea of a "consistently peaceful community of peoples" in his philosophical essay "Project for a perpetual peace". The Enlightenment brought about the first international peace movement in the 19th century, which led to the Hague Peace Conferences in 1899 and 1907.

The aim was to develop principles for the peaceful settlement of international conflicts. The idea behind it is great: the abolition of war as a means of dispute between peoples and instead the establishment of a legal process to resolve conflicts. It did not work back then. The League of Nations failed, and with around 20 wars a year, it is difficult to argue that the UN is more successful today.

"Mr. Chairman and delegates to the United Nations conference on international organisation: Oh, what a wonderful day this can be in history!" With these words, US President Harry S. Truman opened the conference on the establishment of the United Nations.[31]

To this end, diplomats from fifty countries met on 24 April 1945 in San Francisco for the founding conference. With 850 delegates, consultants and other staff – a total of 3,500 people – it was considered the largest international conference of its time to date. The megalomania of multilateralism took its course.

Basis for a better world

On 26 June 1945, the United Nations Charter was solemnly signed by the fifty founding states. US President Harry S. Truman said at the final meeting: "The Charter of the United Nations which you have just signed is a solid structure upon which we can build a better world. History will honour you for it. Between the victory in Europe and the final victory in Japan, in this most destructive of all wars, you have won a victory against war itself. With this Charter the world can begin to look forward to a time when it would be possible for all worthy people to lead a decent life as free human beings".[32]

The words expressed the hopes of the time after more than 50 million deaths in World War II. Such a massacre should never be repeated. However, Truman pointed out that it was not just the fine words in the Charter that mattered but above all their implementation, i.e. the application of the Charter: "If we fail to use it, we shall betray all those who have died in order that we might meet here in freedom and safety to create it. If we seek to use it selfishly – for the advantage of any one nation or any small group of nations – we shall be equally guilty of that betrayal". [33] More than 75 years later, these words sound like a gloomy prophecy, because precisely here in implementation, the UN has repeatedly failed over all these decades largely because of the self-interest of individual states, namely the power to veto: first and foremost the United States, the Soviet Union and China. [34]

China joins the Security Council

After all, the "founding fathers" of the United Nations – Roosevelt, Churchill and Stalin – did not exactly form a "friendship alliance" either, to say the least but wanted to shape the post-war world order according to their power-political ideas and prevent a second "Case of Germany", no matter where, under all conceivable circumstances.

The inclusion of China, which was still quite insignificant at the time, in the Security Council was hardly done out of recognition but simply as a counterweight to the extraordinarily strong Japan, which had not yet surrendered at that time in 1945.[35]

The Security Council is considered the most powerful body of the United Nations because it can pass resolutions that are binding under international law. Paradoxically, it is also regarded as the weakest body because it is literally stalemated by the veto right of its permanent members. How devastating this combination is became apparent soon after the founding of the UN during the Korean conflict. In the current conflict between the United States, Europe, China and Russia, the United Nations is likely to prove equally ineffective because, once again, the fronts at the UN Security Council are all endowed with veto power.

Security Council caught in the veto trap

The Security Council is the only UN body that can pass resolutions that are binding under international law, making it the most powerful organ. According to Article 24 of the UN Charter, it bears "the primary responsibility for the maintenance of international peace and security" and it can also legitimise coercive measures such as sanctions or the use of force. A total of 15 states has seats on the Security Council, including the five permanent members China, France, the United Kingdom, Russia and the USA. The remaining members are elected by the General Assembly for a two-year term, whereby a proportional representation by region is observed. Security Council decisions require a majority of nine votes, including the five permanent members. They thus have a de facto right of veto.[36]

The UN Security Council is the only organ it has that can pass binding resolutions under international law, yet that organ has failed to become a strong contender for peace, justice and humanity, as a direct consequence of the veto principle. The five permanent members of the Security Council – the United States of America, the Russian Federation (since 1991, previously the Soviet Union), the People's Republic of China (since 1971, previously Taiwan), the United Kingdom and France – wanted to ensure at all costs that there could be no decisions against their interests. They therefore stipulated in Article 27 of the UN Charter that no decision can be reached if even one of the members in the Security Council objects. This veto right was due to the circumstances at the time. The founding members were essentially the victorious powers of the Second World War.

The ultimately victorious struggle against the Third Reich had united them – and after the horrors of the war, they remained united in the desire that something like this should never happen again. Although China was not considered a victorious power, it was included in the Council primarily as a counterweight to

Japan; after all, the Japanese had fought side by side with Hitler's Germany and Mussolini's Italy in the Second World War.

The unanimity of the five permanent members of the Security Council quickly dissipated. In the decades of the (First) Cold War, the two arch-enemies, the USA and the Soviet Union, were opposed to each other. Thus, the UN's inability to act was basically already inherent in its DNA. After all, Article 27 of the UN Charter stipulates that a country must abstain from voting if it is itself involved in the conflict that is being submitted to a vote. This means that it cannot exercise any right of veto in this case. However, this presupposes that the permanent members of the UN Security Council must adhere to this rule, which is clearly formulated in the Charter. However, they do not. The Union of Soviet Socialist Republics (USSR), as the Soviet Union was officially known, vetoed the resolution on the invasion of the Czech Republic in 1968, France when it annexed Mayotte in 1976 and the USA in 1986 when it condemned the bombing of Libya, although all three states were undoubtedly involved in each case themselves. Even the attempt to pass a resolution calling for ceasefire in conflict areas in view of the coronavirus pandemic, which is rampant worldwide in 2020, failed for months due to resistance from the USA before an agreement was finally reached.[37]

In other words, the founding members of the highest and only effective body of the United Nations do not themselves abide by their own rules. Rather, in the face of what has probably been the largest global catastrophe since the founding of the United Nations, the 2020/21 pandemic, they placed their own national interests before those of the international community for everyone to see. The right of the strongest supersedes the rights of the community of states. So, it is hardly surprising that there is a lack of respect for the United Nations in many countries around the world, certainly including the USA, China and Russia. Those who accused Russia of a blatant violation of international law in view of the invasion of Ukraine in the spring of 2022 were of course right. But anyone who looks back at the history of the international community in past decades cannot help but accuse the West, and above all the USA, of similar behaviour.

The decisive test of the Korean War

In the battle against Hitler's Germany, Western Europe, North America and the Soviet Union were united in an alliance of convenience. But shortly after the end of the Second World War, the global East-West conflict arose, in which the communist Soviet Union together with the states under its control, including the Eastern Bloc, was the opponent of the free world led by the USA. Faced with the daunting challenge of re-dividing and reshaping Europe and parts of Asia, a fundamental front developed between the communist bloc and the capitalist world.[38]

The East-West conflict formed the fundamental basis for all world politics in the second half of the twentieth century. This is comparable to the China-USA confrontation in the first half of the twenty-first century, not to mention the resurgence of Russia.

The seriousness of this divide became evident as early as 1949, when the then Soviet Union put an end to the US monopoly on nuclear weapons forever with a nuclear test. [39] An arms race began that at times brought the world to the edge of the abyss and has not really ended to this day. In the same year, 1949, Mao

Zedong proclaimed the People's Republic of China; the last president of China, supported by the USA, fled to Taiwan, formerly known as Formosa, and founded the Republic of China. Both developments have played a decisive role in world politics, and especially for the UN for decades until today.

The divided world view – the free world against communism – was the fundamental Achilles' heel of the United Nations from the beginning. The UN was founded to ensure peace in the world but in the decisive body, the Security Council, the then implacable enemies, the United States of America and the Soviet Union, were opponents – both endowed with veto power. There is no denying the analogy to today's situation "USA versus China" with a resurgent Russia.

The Korean question was the first major challenge for the newly established UN. This was intended to show whether the UN would be able to keep the country of Korea in peaceful unity. The Korean War and the fact that the country has been divided into two nations to this day give rise to the conclusion that the United Nations has already failed in this first major decisive test. The reason for this was simple: in the Korean War, the UN gave up its moral authority and neutrality to side with the West in the fight against the Soviet Eastern Bloc.

This unilateral position continues to have an effect today: although the Eastern Bloc has long been history, China and Russia have learned that the international institutions, and above all the UN, side with the West, and thus with the USA, when in doubt. China has derived two strategies from this: firstly, to penetrate the institutions as much as possible with its own Chinese personnel, which has been particularly successful with the World

Health Organisation (WHO), for example, as demonstrated in the 2020/21 pandemic, and secondly, to build "its own" international institutions. An example of this is the Asian Infrastructure Investment Bank (AIIB), a Chinese-led multilateral development bank founded in 2015 by 57 countries, which competes with the World Bank and the International Monetary Fund. The initiative for the foundation in 2015 was prompted by China's dissatisfaction with the supremacy of the US in the International Monetary Fund and the World Bank, which did not reflect a fair distribution of the global balance of power from China's point of view.[40]

Whether or not one interprets the accession of Germany, Great Britain and Italy to the AIIB as bowing to China remains to be seen. In any case, it represents an official recognition of the "International Institutions under Chinese Leadership". China will undoubtedly provide "its" international institutions to Russia in the future.

But back to Korea and the question, why Korea? In World War II, Hitler's Germany had two key allies: Italy and Japan. At that time, Korea belonged to Japan as a protectorate. After the Japanese surrender, the Japanese-ruled Korea was liberated by American and Soviet troops. The US soldiers occupied the land south of the 38th parallel, while the Soviet Union took over the administration of the northern territory. A partition of the country was not initially on the agenda of either of the two occupying powers. Rather, the policy of both sides was to gradually return state power to the country. In doing so, however, both the USA and the Soviet Union made sure early on to encourage the influence of forces that were friendly to them in the country. Then came the big bang for Korea. When it came to reuniting the country, the negotiations were unsuccessful and North and South Korea were divided.

The United Nations played a crucial role in this. The USA handed over the solution to the Korean question to the General Assembly of the United Nations, which initiated the establishment of a "United Nations Temporary Commission on Korea" with Resolution 112 (II). The mandate was "to supervise free and open elections, assist in the withdrawal of the occupying forces, and guide the new political entity to full independence". Even the supervision of the elections went wrong: the Soviet Union and the North Korean administration simply refused entry to the UN-Commission.

The UN was only able to supervise the elections in the south and in August 1948 the southern Republic of Korea was established, which was recognised by the United Nations with resolution 195 (III) as the "lawful and only democratically elected government in Korea". The same thing happened in the north: the Democratic People's Republic of Korea was established, which was not recognised by the UN but recognised by the socialist states under international law. Both Korean states agreed on only one point, in their respective claim to sole representation for the whole of Korea.

Just as the Soviet Union and the Western states squared off against each other on the world stage, the fronts between North and South Korea were equally hardened. Just like on the large scale, there was also a lot of armament "on the small scale" and after various border disputes on the 38th parallel, North Korean troops invaded South Korean soil. Whether the USSR was behind this remained unclear but it seemed to be certain that they at least knew about it. On 25 On 25 June 1950, on the initiative of the United States, the United Nations convened the UN Security Council; the USA submitted a draft resolution condemning North Korea as an "aggressor" ("Act of Unprovoked Aggression"). The moderate formulation of a "Breach of Peace" was adopted with a call to North Korea to stop the fighting and withdraw its armed forces.

The resolution was passed 9-0, with former Yugoslavia abstaining. What was remarkable, however, was a completely different fact: the Soviet Union was not present at all in this vote. It thus launched an attempt to simply ignore, or one could even say discredit, the United Nations through absence.

The background was obvious: the United States had achieved supremacy in the UN Security Council because all the victorious powers of World War II represented in the Council, except for the USSR and China, had sided with the United States of America. Today's China and today's Russia may not be the best of friends but their historic bond in the United Nations Security Council continues to this day – if only because they see a common enemy in the USA. At the time, the Soviet Union and China could have rejected the condemnation of North Korea with their veto power but they preferred to boycott the UN instead. Exactly this case was not envisaged in the UN Charter in the first place.

In this regard, Article 27 III of the UN Charter states: "Decisions of the Security Council on all other matters shall be made by an affirmative vote of nine members including the concurring votes of the permanent members; provided that, in decisions under Chapter VI, and under paragraph 3 of Article 52, a party to a dispute shall abstain from voting". Not being there at all was simply not part of the agenda. At least the question was discussed whether the absence of the USSR should be seen as a veto or an abstention.

On 27 June 1950, two days after the first meeting, a second meeting of the UN Security Council on Korea was held, at which it was stated that North Korea had not complied with the resolution of 25 June 1950. Consequently, the US introduced a new draft that was supposed to allow them to intervene militarily in Korea. UN members were asked to "provide aid to the Republic of Korea to furnish such assistance to the Republic of Korea as may be necessary to repel the armed attack and to restore international peace and security in the area".

At this point in time, the "region" was apparently referring to South Korea but later it turned out to be fatal that precisely this was not formulated in the text and therefore also allowed the interpretation that the whole of Korea could be meant. Irrespective of this, the then US President Harry S. Truman had long since set the air and naval forces in motion in the direction of Korea at the time of the UN resolution. The US government wanted its military operation in Korea, which was not just planned but was already being prepared, to be approved by the United Nations in retrospect. And they did.

How seriously the US government took their military action can be deduced from the fact that the Seventh Fleet had also already received deployment orders to protect Taiwan from communist China. With the "blessing" of the UN, the US obviously wanted to prevent both the intervention of Soviet and Chinese troops. From the US point of view, it was a politically clever move to use the UN as a puppet of US military intervention. But of course, this was devastating for the credibility of the United Nations as an independent institution. This is even more true since the resolution in question passed the UN Security Council – after all, the USSR at the time continued to pursue its strategy of ignoring the United Nations through absence.

The joint US/UN war

What happened afterwards can probably only be assessed as a kind of joint US/UN war. The United States of America set the strategy, commanded the armed forces, broke the UN Charter as far as it seemed expedient to them, and repeatedly abused the United Nations to cloak their own actions in the guise of neutrality, as action collectively desired by the international community for the establishment and safeguarding of peace. Never before and never since has a single nation so brazenly abused the United Nations as the United States did in the Korean conflict.

One thing must be credited to the USA. however: At that time, they saw themselves as the leader of the free world, which had to defend itself tooth and nail against the rising military strength of the communist bloc. It was probably the fear that communism, rampant in the Soviet Union and China, could become so strong that it would subjugate the free world. To prevent this, the USA was apparently willing to resort to any means – including abuse of the UN. When assessing the situation at the time, however, it should be borne in mind that the fear of an aggressive communist expansionist strategy controlled by Moscow and Peking (later named Beijing) was by no means akin to the USA alone but dominated practically the entire Western world and thus also the United Nations, in which the USA's Western allies were overwhelmingly represented. North Korea's attack on the south of the country seemed to fit exactly into this thought pattern and was rated accordingly. True to the motto "nip it in the bud", the prevailing impression was probably that, if the communists in North Korea were not kept at bay, the communist bloc might be encouraged to spread globally.

One may assume that the same front still exists today (or again) in the United Nations: the USA and the West on one side, China and Russia on the other. For all Europe's primarily economic rapprochement with China in recent decades, the European states within the UN will certainly not oppose the USA and speak out in favour of China UN even today. This would probably not even have happened under America-first President Donald Trump and will certainly not happen under his successor Joe Biden, who is driving the rapprochement with Europe.

At that time, on 7 July 1950, UN Security Council Resolution 84 made it clear that all troops deployed in Korea should bear the UN flag. It was even more remarkable, however, that the resolution did not set any specific goal whatsoever. Should the North Korean groups be pushed back beyond the 38th parallel, should South Korea be protected from renewed attacks, should North Korea be occupied or should the whole country be reunified? There was simply no decision on it but the UN pursued all these points in that order.

The question of whether the United Nations was even entitled to reunite two states remained unanswered. It was also ultimately irrelevant to the US military advance under the Commander-in-Chief of the American Forces in East Asia, General Douglas MacArthur, with the support of troops from 16 states including South Korea. The chain of command, however, spoke for itself: MacArthur received his instructions from the US government, to which he also constantly sent his situation reports. In a second step, the UN was kept informed by the US government.[41]

At first, everything indicated that US/UN troops would win. Victory meant that the North Korean troops would be forced to withdraw to the north whereby the border would be secured. This would have restored the situation exactly as it was before the North Koreans invaded the south of the country.

But General Douglas MacArthur decided otherwise. Of course, with the support of large parts of the US government, he chose the reunification of Korea as his target and decided to invade North Korea. Crossing the 38th parallel to the north was not sanctioned by any UN resolution but there was also no resolution at the United Nations that explicitly contradicted this goal. A UN mission had been approved but the objective was simply left open. Whether this was due to a lack of professionalism or whether the ulterior motive from the beginning was to use the mission for an attack on North Korea could never be determined. Possibly both were true.

In any case, the assessment that neither the Soviet Union nor China would oppose the US/UN advance proved to be a fatal error, triggering a brutal proxy war between the two major political-military blocs in Korea, as it was later repeated in an even more savage war in Vietnam.

In the case of Korea, the US/UN complex also completely misjudged the behaviour of the People's Republic of China. China's

Foreign Minister Chou En-lai had issued warnings in advance but the US government did not take them seriously enough, assuming a bluff. Since China did not intervene right from the start, it was considered extremely unlikely that China would intervene afterwards. Why should China intervene to support the USSR? In addition, the prevailing opinion was that the People's Republic of China would not argue with the UN, as it also had to decide on the question of the status of Taiwan – that is, from the perspective of the PRC, the old and hated China. So, the assessment of granting China some kind of respect at the United Nations was already wrong then – it is likely to prove equally wrong today in the race for supremacy in 2049.

However, another UN resolution seemed appropriate for the US/UN troops to cross the 38th parallel. The only problem was that by this time, the Soviet Union had given up its UN boycott and returned to the Security Council. It was obvious that the USSR (together with China) would veto any decision to send Western soldiers into North Korea. Faced with this predictable situation, the US administration reached into its "bag of tricks": Knowing that it would not get through in the Security Council, it shifted the decision-making process on North Korea without further ado to the General Assembly, which at that time was dominated by US-friendly states and in which there was no right of veto. Once again, the United States was playing with the United Nations as if it owned it – and the UN let it happen.

In September 1950, the United States introduced a draft resolution to the UN General Assembly indirectly allowing the UN military to enter North Korea with the aim of uniting the country and securing peace throughout Korea. To achieve this goal, the "necessary measures" were to be taken, which could be interpreted as an invasion permit. With a few amendments, this resolution 376 (V) was passed by the UN General Assembly on 7 October 1950 by 45:5 votes with seven abstentions. The resolution provided for the creation of a united, independent and democratic Korea following the victorious deployment of US/UN troops.[42]

This approach was in no way compatible with the UN Charter, so one could speak of an illegal UN resolution as the starting signal for the Korean War. According to the Charter, all decisions in the event of a breach of peace are the sole responsibility of the Security Council. The General Assembly may only pass resolutions on this if the Security Council does not deal with them and, above all, the General Assembly resolutions are not binding under any circumstances; they are merely recommendations for action.

But even assuming everything around the UN resolution of 7 October 1950 had been legitimate, it would still only have legitimised the US/UN measures after the event. General MacArthur was in fact already authorised by the US government on 27 September 1950 to "cross the 38th parallel and destroy the North Korean army".[43]

China versus US/UN pact

The People's Republic of China threw a spanner in the works of the victorious US/UN complex. As soon as General MacArthur crossed the 38th parallel, China ordered its troops from Dongbei Pingyuang into North Korea. After China had previously issued open warnings, MacArthur's military advance could only be classified as an equally open provocation.

Moreover, China's President Mao Zedong evidently feared that "the reactionaries here and abroad would become cocky when the enemy troops march on the Yalu River". The 813-kilometre long Jalu is the border river between China and North Korea.[44]

With the mobilisation of China, the Korean conflict outgrew its regional boundaries and threatened to spread to mainland Asia. Against this backdrop, the UN Security Council invited China to a discussion that took place on 28 November 1950 in New York. The mutual accusations of the superpowers never ended. China accused the US of aggression, the Soviet Union wanted American aggression against China to be condemned, and the US asked China to withdraw from Korea. Every proposal failed in the UN Security Council due to the veto of the other side.

Since the Security Council had become incapable of acting with the renewed involvement of the Soviet Union, the USA shifted once more to the strategy of bringing about UN decisions in the General Assembly. For this purpose, resolution 377 (V) "Uniting for Peace" was passed on November 3, 1950 (with 52 votes to 5 with two abstentions).[45] It introduced five innovations:

1. If the Security Council is deadlocked by a veto, a decision can be delegated to the General Assembly, which is then entitled to decide on breaches of the peace and "to be able to make recommendations for collective measures, including the use of armed forces".

2. An emergency meeting could be convened within 24 hours with a majority in the Security Council or in the General Assembly.

3. An observation group can be set up for regions that pose a threat to international peace.

4. Each member state of the United Nations should reserve part of its armed forces for international missions.

5. It is planned to set up an advisory committee to propose measures to maintain international peace and security.

But it did not help, the USA could not be victorious in Korea, not even with the help of the United Nations. As this became increasingly more obvious, the USA, as well as the UN in Korea, placed an emphasis on humanitarian aid. On 1 December 1950, the United Nations Reconstruction Agency was finally set up to help the people who had fled the North Korean invasion and were threatened by the Chinese invasion. However, even this aid could hardly be provided due to China's military successes, so that from Spring 1951 onwards the soldiers were required to give relief supplies and food to the civilian population.

Shortly after the outbreak of the Korean War, US President Harry S. Truman announced that the use of nuclear bombs against China could no longer be ruled out. Anyone who believed that the USA had refrained from these weapons of destruction after the nuclear bombs were dropped on Hiroshima and Nagasaki was mistaken. Particularly the UK government opposed these considerations in the strongest possible terms. India proposed admitting China to the UN Security Council but this failed at the time because of the US government.

In the so-called "Ceasefire Group" of the UN, India, Canada and Iran tried to sound out conditions for a ceasefire. The group drew up a proposal that included "a ceasefire, the withdrawal of all foreign forces, the formation of a Korean government based on UN principles, and the formation of a UN led body with the participation of the USA, the USSR, the United Kingdom and China to solve all the problems of East Asia, including the representation of Taiwan and China in the UN". The concept looked promising but failed when the UN, on the initiative of the USA, condemned the People's Republic of China as an aggressor and even threatened to impose sanctions.

Chaos reigned until General Douglas MacArthur – once again – took over the reins. In March 1951 he made a statement on his own initiative in which he threatened China with the destruction of its industrial and military facilities and the use of nuclear weapons. The general was then quickly recalled by the US government but it became clear how close the world was to the abyss.[46]

In this situation, the USA could hardly have counted on the support of other countries. The European countries in particular would presumably not have sent more troops to Asia for fear of weakening their own defensive power against the USSR.

The Chinese leadership will not have forgotten the US nuclear threat at that time until today. It will therefore presumably be extremely cautious about allowing a scenario to develop that could even provoke the threat of nuclear military action on the part of the USA. But at the same time, China has long since begun to prepare for a new military confrontation with the USA. As the historical example of the Korean conflict shows, just as China supported the then Soviet Union in the Korean conflict, the Chinese government can hope for support from Russia today – not only at the UN negotiating table. It is true that the People's Republic of China today acts with considerably more diplomacy than, say, Russia, so as not to alienate the West as an economic partner or even be exposed to Western sanctions but in the UN Security Council, for example, depending on the situation at hand, an abstention is enough to turn decisions one way or the other.

The longest war on earth

In view of the stagnation of the Korean War with no prospect of a victory for either side, the first negotiations on an armistice began in the summer of 1951. At this time at the latest, the great moment of the United Nations could have arrived. However, there was no great moment. The UN did not even get a serious negotiating mandate. However, this did not prevent them from giving themselves a particularly good report card some two years later: In Resolution 711 (VII) of the UN General Assembly of 28 August 1953, the "active participation of the United Nations in the Korean War was promptly acknowledged as a contribution to world peace".

In fact, however, the superpowers were irreconcilably opposed to each other in the negotiations until the summer of 1953. The United Nations made no significant contribution to the contentious issues of the demarcation line, the establishment of a demilitarised zone and the withdrawal of foreign forces. Only on the important question of the repatriation of prisoners of war did the UN General Assembly, in December 1952, pass Resolution 610 (VII) on the establishment of a commission of neutral states, which, however, remained largely ineffective.[47]

It was only when the Russian dictator Josef Stalin died, and Dwight D. Eisenhower was elected president in the USA that the peace negotiations finally made rapid progress. A Ceasefire Agreement was concluded on 27 July 1953, which largely restored the status quo prior to the war. By then, nearly four million people had lost their lives in the Korean War, around three quarters of them civilians. In its resolution 711 (VII) of 28 August 1953, the UN General Assembly stated that the Ceasefire Agreement was essential for the restoration of international peace and recommended that all parties participate in the peace conference.[48]

Despite the armistice, the Korean War has not formally ended to this day. The north and the south are still separated. South Korean President Moon Jae-in and North Korean government leader Kim Jong-un have been trying, since 2018, to officially end what has been, in some respects, the longest war on earth.

In addition to other challenges, the USA is once again standing in the way. This includes, on the one hand, the question of the withdrawal of US troops from South Korea, and, on the other hand, the US demand for military and, above all, nuclear disarmament in North Korea. South Korea's priority is rapprochement and reconciliation, while the USA's primary concern is military supremacy. And the People's Republic of China is basically still standing by North Korea today as its only more or less ally, for example when it comes to cyber war, as described elsewhere in this book.

Vietnam followed Korea

The Korean War of the 1950s was followed by the Vietnam War as the most significant theatre of war in the 1960s. The role of the UN can be described in just a few words: the United Nations had no active role in the Vietnam War because, firstly, the superpowers fought the conflict among themselves and, secondly, neither North nor South Vietnam was represented in the UN. The Vietnam War, however, exemplifies the clash between the USA, on the one hand, and China and Russia, or at that time the USSR, on the other.

The Vietnam War had its roots in the nineteenth century when France placed the country under colonial rule as part of French Indochina. Japan occupied the area during the Second World War. Immediately afterwards, France attempted to restore its colonial rule in the First Indochina War from 1946 to 1954 but was unsuccessful. As a result of the French defeat, Vietnam was divided in 1954 into the communist North Vietnam with its capital Hanoi and the Western-backed South Vietnam with its capital Saigon. This was the starting point for the Vietnam War, also known as the Second Indochina War. It started as a civil war after the division but expanded into a proxy war between communism and the US-dominated West from 1964 onwards.

From February 1965, US President Lyndon B. Johnson bombed North Vietnam, and a month later he sent increasingly more ground troops into the country. In return, the Soviet Union and the People's Republic of China supported North Vietnam. This left the veto powers in the UN Security Council at war with each other and rendered the UN powerless. A cruel massacre took its course over the years.

The USA used the chemical defoliant Agent Orange in the fight against the North Korean-controlled National Front for the Liberation of South Vietnam (NFB, better known as Viet Cong) to render any camouflage of the enemy fighters through the dense jungle difficult. Agent Orange was sprayed from aircraft on such a large scale that hundreds of thousands of people fell ill from it. An estimate of the Red Cross in 2002 put the number of Vietnamese with health damage from the after-effects of Agent Orange at one million, including about 100,000 children with congenital malformations. Damage to the embryo, cancer and immune deficiencies are typical consequences of dioxins, whose particularly toxic form TCDD (tetrachlorodibenzodioxin) was a component of Agent Orange.

It was not until 1968 that Johnson stopped the bombing, and his successor as US president, Richard Nixon, gradually withdrew US troops from 1969 onwards, even agreeing to a ceasefire with North Vietnam in January 1973. By 1 May 1975, North Vietnamese soldiers had completely conquered the South, ending the war and unifying the country. By the time this happened, 1.3 million Vietnamese fighters had died; the civilians killed are estimated at between two and five million people.

UN Secretary-General Sithu U Thant spoke of one of the "most barbaric wars in history", described this situation as "very urgent, very critical" and made several attempts, between 1961 and 1971, to bring about peace.[49] By means of shuttle diplomacy –

Geneva, Cairo, London, Moscow, Washington – U Thant tried to bring about a joint commitment by the conflicting parties to the Geneva Agreement of 1954.[50] This would have brought about peace in the country but at the same time accepted the division of the nation into the communist north and the more westernised south under the reign of Emperor Bao Dai, the 13th and last emperor of the Vietnamese Nguyen dynasty.[51] The Geneva Agreement, however, was primarily aimed at decolonising the Vietnam / Laos / Cambodia region from French rule and was therefore inappropriate from the outset for the proxy war between communism and the Western powers in Vietnam. The impression was that the UN was behind the times but it had nothing better to offer in view of the stalemate in the Security Council.

Sithu U Thant's attempts at peace were honourable and certainly befitted his position but they highlighted the paralysis of the United Nations. Finally, the UN Secretary-General himself had to admit that the Vietnam conflict was outside a "UN mandate" because North and South Vietnam were not member countries. It was tantamount to a declaration of failure of the United Nations.

When analysing the resurgence of China in the 2020s on the way to the centenary of the People's Republic in 2049, and the resurgence of Russia, one should always be mindful of the proxy wars in Korea and in Vietnam and the inglorious role of the United Nations in them. Modern China will not allow the UN to be instrumentalised by the USA again. Conversely, however, China stands little chance of being able to harness the UN to its own cart. For Russia, the UN is only significant as far as they can use their veto power to prevent a binding condemnation of their country.

The confrontation between the United States, China and Russia means that a peaceful agreement in consultation with the international community of states and in the spirit of multilateralism is not even on the horizon.

Multilateralism has had its day

It must be noted that multilateralism has not only been on the brink of collapse since 2020 and that it has basically failed. After the USA proclaimed the primacy of the nation state in 2016 with a rigorous America First policy, many other countries followed suit. In Europe, the refugee crisis that has been simmering since 2015 has long threatened the unity of the EU. The Brexit at the beginning of 2020, after the UK's having been member for 47 years, has been a caesura that hardly anybody previously thought possible. The 2020/21 pandemic could have been a salutary shock but instead it has led to rifts everywhere. The inauguration of the US government under President Joe Biden at the beginning of 2021 at least gave rise to the hope that there will be more international cohesion in what is presumably the next great challenge for humanity: averting the climate catastrophe. But whether it will go beyond hope seems questionable. In any case, during the pandemic, the USA under Biden maintained a strict export ban on vaccines for months, even for those vaccines for which there was no approval in the USA itself.[52] China, on the other hand, offered vaccine serums worldwide – but many countries rejected them due to doubts about their efficacy.[53] This situation from the year 2021 illustrated once again how China presented itself as a global player that wants to help almost the entire world with a great sense of responsibility – the beginning of a new world order.

Under the leadership of the USA, the superpowers have been regrouping since 2016 to a greater extent than at any time since the Second World War. The United States of America dropped out of multilateralism and declared itself once again the ruler of the world with its "America first" strategy. Joe Biden's victory in 2020 did bring the USA back into the international institutions – but with the unchanged claim to be the "number one" in the world, far beyond its own territory. After the collapse of the Soviet Union, Russia had tried to regain its strength. China, in particular, visibly moved from its alleged obscurity into the limelight. For a long time, China was seen only as an extended and above all cheap workbench of the Western industrial nations and as a gigantic sales market but it has increasingly become a political heavyweight.

This was symbolically demonstrated at the 75th UN General Assembly in 2020, which was held only online due to the coronavirus pandemic. While the USA stood for unilateralism, China functioned as the defender of multilateralism. "The baton of history has been passed to our generation," said China's leader Xi Jinping, and it sounded as if China had accepted that baton.[54]

For years, the emergence of these global power centres was contrasted in Europe by the disintegration of the European Union. In other words, Europe's role on the world stage will probably become increasingly smaller in the 2020s, although the roots of world politics lie in the "Old Continent".

Only Russia's attack on Ukraine in 2022 abruptly brought Europe back into the focus of world politics. The European Union was suddenly more popular than ever before – but primarily as a protective wall against Russian aggression and with the expectation of being defended by the EU and above all by NATO in the event of a Russian attack. Thus, it was not so much Europe's independence as its alignment with the USA as a protective power against Russia that attracted new member candidates to the EU.

The end of multilateralism

The foundations of today's diplomacy date back to the Congress of Vienna in the nineteenth century. Formal, multilateral diplomacy was also established there. Multilateral (from Latin multus "much"; latus "side") means "multifaceted". In international law, the term multilateral is used when three or more states – or other subjects of international law – collaborate, in principle on an equal footing, for example, to maintain diplomatic relations or conclude treaties.

Since then, multilateralism has gained in importance over decades and ousted the previously customary, mostly purely intergovernmental – bilateral – diplomacy in many areas. This also quickly gave rise to numerous international organisations, the United Nations certainly being one of the most important of these. However, its basic idea, the equal rights of all nations represented in the UN, was built on sand from the very beginning. Even if the Security Council was a multilateral organ, it undermined the equality of all states from the very beginning, driven by the East-West conflict between communism and the Western world that overshadowed everything for decades.

The later enlargement of the UN by developing and emerging countries revealed new strands of conflict, especially between poor and rich countries. Since 2015, the global resurgence of nationalism as a countermovement to multilateralism has shaken the foundation of the United Nations. Since 2016 at the latest, the gradual decline of multilateralism became apparent, driven at the time by the election of Donald Trump as US president and the rise of national forces in many other countries, especially in Europe. It is probably naïve to believe that multilateralism will revive as before with Joe Biden as US President. On the contrary, the coronavirus pandemic in 2020 has reinforced a national mindset almost everywhere in the world. Even within the European Union, there were temporary border closures out of the realisation that national legislation, and thus also the measures to combat the pandemic, end at their own national borders.

What had been developed into a stable multilateral cooperation system over decades, at the cost of millions of lives lost in both world wars, was now threatening to fall by the wayside again, sacrificed to the national delusions of grandeur of new "leaders". Those who had believed that globalisation, multilateralism and worldwide challenges had produced a new type of leader, a better elite, who could think globally and in the interest of all, found themselves bitterly disappointed.

The appeal for radical reform of the entire UN system expressed in the study of the Independent Commission on Multilateralism in 2016 "The Multilateral System and its Future", did not go unheard but the reform was poorly implemented. The report, which identified ten clear principles to revitalise multilateralism, was intended to provide a basis for making the United Nations fit for the 2020s. One insight was that multilateralism cannot be managed with ever more complexity. But – complexity – is precisely what has always characterised the UN, and it is not on the wane, but rather on the increase, as is to be feared, even in the 2020s.[55] However, it was neither Russia nor China that was the first to shun the UN, it was the USA.

The US shuns international organisations

The United States of America, once an enormously proud co-founder of the UN – after all, the then US-President Harry S. Truman held both the inaugural and founding speeches in 1945 – has increasingly distanced itself from the United Nations over the years. One can attribute this to forgetting the 50 million casualties of the Second World War. It can also be attributed to the spread of nationalist ideology since 2015, not only in the USA, and the shift to the right in the world. However, one can also consider the obvious weaknesses of the United Nations as a reason for the USA to turn away from the UN. A good example of this is the United Nations Human Rights Council.

The administration of US President George W. Bush voted against the establishment of the Human Rights Council in 2006 – long before the egomaniac Donald Trump took office for four years. At the time, John Bolton was American ambassador to the United Nations, a particularly harsh critic of the UN. Bolton later became national security advisor to US President Trump, whose "America first" strategy took precedence over any multilateralism. In 2021, after the withdrawal of US troops from Afghanistan, Bolton warned that Taliban terrorists could gain possession of nuclear weapons.[56]

However, it would be too easy to simply attribute the US rejection of the UN Human Rights Council to American nationalism. In fact, the Council, which was established in 2006, has serious structural weaknesses. The UN General Assembly elects the 47 members of the Human Rights Council for three-year terms. In 2019, these included Cuba, Congo and Venezuela, three countries where human rights organisations have repeatedly denounced extremely serious human rights violations. When, to put it mildly, suspects sit on the bench to investigate misconduct all over the world, one must indeed seriously question the usefulness of such an institution. After all, human rights are one of the core issues of the United Nations; any weakness in this regard strikes at the heart of the entire organisation.

In 2017, US Ambassador to the UN Nikki Haley urged three reforms at a meeting in Geneva. She demanded that the Council reduce its focus on Israel. She also wanted to reduce the number of votes needed to expel members for blatant human rights violations. Moreover, there were to be fewer speeches and resolutions.[57] There was no majority on the first two points At least the last point resulted in a work task: The Human Rights Council was concerned with figuring out how to talk less and produce less paper in the future. The envisaged reduction of bureaucracy, if successful, would certainly be good for the Council. But this does not change the fundamental deficiency that states that persistently commit serious human rights violations continue to be members of the body. Worse still, there was no majority in the UN to abolish this almost absurd situation until 2021 – and probably there will not be any after that either.

US President Joe Biden is obviously following the path of Trump's predecessor Barack Obama, under whom he served as Vice President from 2009 to 2014. In his last speech to the United Nations in September 2016, Obama had described the role of the US with rhetorical adroitness as follows: "Many people believe that all problems were either caused by Washington or could be solved by Washington".

The ambivalence of the USA in its relationship with the UN and other international organisations is undoubtedly related, among other things, to the fact that the once only true superpower in the world views the apparently unstoppable rise of the People's Republic of China as a global power with the greatest concern and apparently believes that it is better to defend itself in direct confrontation than in the UN, where China can easily use its veto power to obstruct everything. This also applies to Russia. As early as 2018, the German foreign minister had proclaimed an "alliance of multilateralists". In autumn 2019, around 50 states convened for the first time on the occasion of the UN General Assembly in New York. It was a desperate attempt of an informal circle to counteract the dwindling influence of international organisations and the crumbling validity of global rules, for example, in the area of trade. It was also an admission that multilateral institutions such as the United Nations are in danger of losing their relevance in view of the global conflict between the USA, Russia and China.

EU "comeback" since 24 February 2022

The Russian invasion of Ukraine on 24 February 2022 has given the European Union a boost that hardly anyone could have imagined a day earlier.

On the one hand, it has reinforced the unity of the EU member states. Within a noticeably short time, there was agreement to condemn the invasion, to support Ukraine with military equipment and to impose sanctions against the Kremlin. Whereas in the previous waves of refugees from Syria or Afghanistan, for example, there had been hopeless disagreements, the refugees from Ukraine were welcomed with open arms in practically all countries – both by politicians and by the population.

On the other hand, there has been a veritable run on the European Union (and NATO) by countries outside the EU to escape the fangs of Russia. Not surprisingly, Ukraine wanted to become an EU member by means of a "new special procedure". The "special procedure" meant that the admission should take place within the shortest possible time. However, the applications of Georgia and the Republic of Moldova for EU membership were all the more surprising. Georgia's head of government Irakli Garibashvili clarified: "Georgia is a "European state". Geographically, Georgia is undoubtedly located in the Middle East, more precisely in the Caucasus but its people often refer to it as the "balcony of Europe". Georgia has been a member of the Council of Europe since 2009. However, new applications can never reckon with a quick admission to the EU. As a rule, it takes one to one and a half years for the EU Commission to make an initial assessment. The EU countries ultimately decide on accession to the European Union.[58]

At that time, when the new applications arrived in Brussels in spring 2022, five states already had official status as candidates for EU membership. The EU grants this official status to countries that have applied for membership that has been unanimously adopted by the Council of the European Union following a positive recommendation by the European Commission. Negotiations were already underway with two of them, Turkey and Montenegro. No accession negotiations had been initiated with Northern Macedonia, Serbia and Albania by the time this book was published. Moreover, Bosnia-Herzegovina applied for membership in 2016.[59]The rapid accession of new countries called for in view of the Russian attack on Ukraine in 2022 would, however, be diametrically opposed to the actions of the European institutions to date. Turkey is an example of this. The country joined the European Customs Union in 1996 and has been a candidate for EU membership since 1999. Accession negotiations started on 3 October 2005, after the European Council had expressed its support on 17 December 2004, whereupon the European Parliament, whose decision is not legally binding on the Heads of State and Government, had also advocated the start of accession negotiations by a large majority on 15 December 2004. However, in the summer of 2017, the accession option was no longer considered realistic.

There was an extensive list of concerns. It is probably in the eye of the beholder whether Turkey should be assigned to Asia or Europe. The argument that Turkey, as a Muslim country, is not culturally part of Christian Europe can be countered by saying that the EU is not defined by religion. In addition, there were economic concerns due to low economic power and a low level of development in a comparatively large population of 83 million.

Supporters countered that Turkey has had an influence on European history for 500 years and has characterised itself as European at least since Mustafa Kemal Atatürk, the founder of the modern Republic of Turkey, which emerged from the Ottoman Empire after the First World War. But the twelfth president of the republic since 2014, Recep Tayyip Erdoğan, has increasingly restricted democratic and rule-of-law standards in Turkey after an initial phase of democratisation. One may discover in this a whole series of parallels to Russia under Vladimir Putin, who also initially turned towards Europe in a more cosmopolitan and Western-oriented way before the new cold and then hot war broke out. Similar to the Russians, the Turks look back on a long history of relevance before newer powers such as the USA and the European Union, China and, more recently, Russia again became the main actors on the world stage. The Turkic people comprise around 180 to 200 million people with about 40 ethnic groups in Central and Western Asia as well as in Siberia and Eastern Europe. Today's Turkey is at best a middle power but many of Erdoğan's appearances and statements suggest that the country is keen to take a frontline role in the world. There are some indications that Turkey will not leave it at this wish in the long run but will become active in creating more relevance for itself. Turkey has been a member of NATO since 1952 and provides the military alliance with the second largest number of active soldiers after the USA.[60]

A run on NATO

As a result of Putin's war against Ukraine, some surprising demands have been addressed to the EU, but there has also been a run on NATO. The two northern countries Finland and Sweden, which have always emphasised their neutrality or non-alignment, began to seriously discuss NATO membership in the spring of 2022. Finland, which shares a 1300-kilometre border with Russia, had maintained a good neighbourly relationship for decades. Finland even coordinated important foreign and security policy decisions with Moscow. The term "Finlandisation" has become a political buzzword describing the influence that a powerful state exerts on a smaller neighbouring country and its policies. In return, non-aligned Finland was able to secure some advantages such as brisk economic trade with Russia.[61]

But since 24 February 2022, freedom of alliance was no longer a matter of course in Finland, nor in Sweden. In a letter, the Kremlin demanded security guarantees from both countries. Russia's threat that joining NATO would have "serious military and political consequences" for the two countries has tended to encourage the move towards the Western military alliance. Against the background of the significantly deteriorated security situation in the wake of the war against Ukraine, Sweden and Finland had unceremoniously held a joint military exercise in the Baltic Sea. But like a forewarning, four Russian SU-27 and SU-24 fighter jets entered the airspace over Sweden during the exercise.[62]

No one has declared World War III

After the First World War with 20 million losses, the international community founded the League of Nations with a single goal: to prevent a Second World War. Unfortunately, the League of Nations failed. Around 20 years later, preparations began for the Second World War, which cost over 50 million lives. The

United Nations Organisation was established to prevent a Third World War. Has it succeeded so far? That is arguable. Fortunately, no one has yet declared World War III.

Yet war has long since not just been underway. Worse yet, it has been on the rise. Today more wars are raging around the world than ever before. War is rampant on five out of seven continents. The global number of military conflicts has been rising steadily for years, as has the number of victims and refugees who want to escape the wars and save their lives. Even during the biggest global catastrophe of the twenty-first century to date, the global spread of the coronavirus, the UN was unable to pass even one binding resolution on a global ceasefire for several months; not to mention the frequently criticised action taken by the World Health Organization (WHO), which is part of the UN, in the face of the pandemic. On the contrary, the idea of multilateralism, i.e. coordinated joint action by the international community, has been more in question since the beginning of the 2020s than during the Cold War – or should we say at the time of the "First Cold War", if we classify the front between China and the USA as the "Second Cold War"? Incidentally, the Russian invasion of Ukraine in 2022 showed how quickly a supposedly "cold war" can turn hot and claim lives. But if multilateralism cannot be advanced "just like that", it is high time to think about new forms of state cooperation at the international level.

Angela Merkel's new world order

Already at the World Economic Forum 2019 in Davos, Switzerland, the former German Chancellor Angela Merkel, who at the time was considered the "most powerful woman in world politics", pleaded for a new world order. Her appeal at the time left nothing to be desired in terms of clarity: the fragmentation of the world order could only be prevented if reforms ensured that the institutions reflected the current balance of power, no longer just that of the Second World War. Many institutions had proven to have lengthy administrative procedures.

For example, the capital increase of the World Bank decided in 2018 was long overdue because the economic balance of power has shifted. "If an existing system reacts far too slowly to this, the consequence is of course that others make themselves felt with new institutions", said German Chancellor Angela Merkel in Davos. She was referring to the Asian Investment Bank and other new formats with China at the centre. She understood this as a "warning signal",

saying that the need for a new order was also the result of completely new challenges. As an example of such a challenge, she mentioned digitalisation, above all artificial intelligence and the handling of confidential data. But answers have also been lacking in the areas of genetic engineering and bioethics. It is a matter of developing a new architecture in order to be able to face these new developments together."But that presupposes that we do not ruin the existing order to such an extent that no one believes in new parameters anymore", said Angela Merkel. There was no viable alternative to a multilateral order.[63]

In 2019, the then Chancellor already addressed what had long since ceased to be news by that time but what had become clearer than ever before in the coronavirus pandemic of 2020/21: there has been a crisis of multilateralism for decades, and it is to be feared that this will continue in the 2020s. The new world order seems more likely to consist of blocs clustered around the three superpowers, with China undoubtedly the most emergent of the three.

Russia on the fence

Russia is on the fence. In Europe, the Western world, under the guidance of the USA, has expanded eastwards over the years with the EU and NATO. There is hardly any room left for Russia in Europe; the attack on Ukraine in 2022 marked an attempt to reverse this development or at least put a stop to it.

On the other hand, there is China's rapidly growing claim to power. In this situation, Russia under Vladimir Putin has fought for an independent position. Putin had taken office in 2000 with the agenda of an economic reformer. "The principles of strengthening the state and market reforms" were on the agenda. In the ten years after Putin took office, Russia's economic output grew in absolute terms from $260 billion to $1.9 trillion, an eightfold increase. Unemployment fell to five percent; incomes rose three times faster than productivity. In 1999, six per cent of Russians had to live on less than two dollars a day; in 2013, this poverty was almost completely eradicated.[64] However, after more than a decade of advancement, Russia has been more likely to find itself in a phase of stagnation again in the early 2020s. Since Putin's return to the Kremlin in 2012, economic development has been sobering. Thus, the economy grew just between 1.5 and 2 per cent per annum in the years before 2020. Despite the economic challenges, Russia seems determined not to relinquish its resurgent claim as a superpower once again, which suffered greatly from the collapse of the Eastern bloc after the Cold War but rather to expand it further – including the conspicuous demonstration of power with the invasion of Ukraine in February 2022, which in many respects was a miscalculation.

Thus, the Russian invasion simultaneously revived NATO and brought the Americans back to Europe, who "in fact" only wanted to take care of China and the Indo-Pacific. Moreover, the invasion has achieved something that French President Emmanuel Macron has been unable to achieve over the last five years, namely, to create a Europe of defence.

For the United States of America, it has been clear since the beginning of 2022 that it must not only look to East Asia but also keep an eye on Europe in order to prevent its decline as a superpower. US President Donald Trump made it abundantly clear that the USA claims to be the only real superpower on earth that can assert its interests anywhere in the world, through political pressure, economic measures such as tariffs or sanctions and, if necessary, military intervention. US President Joe Biden formulates this claim more elegantly, as did Donald Trump's predecessor Barack Obama, but the moderate rhetoric does not mitigate the claim as such.

USA vs. China: Russia gets in on the act

For decades, the Chinese government's actions have been geared towards a particular deadline: 1 October 2049. On this day, the People's Republic of China will celebrate its centenary. President Xi Jinping is determined to make his country number one in the world by then: economically, technologically and militarily. To achieve his goal, he therefore has just under 30 years in which he must succeed in overtaking the USA in order to win the day. With this historic date in mind, China will spare no measures to assert its claim to world power. Anyone analysing Chinese development must always be aware of this unbending objective to which everything in China must be subordinated.

The celebrations of the seventieth anniversary of the People's Republic of China on 1 October 2019 impressively or shockingly demonstrated the strategy, depending on one's point of view: No force "can ever undermine our great motherland's status, or stop the Chinese people and the Chinese nation from marching forward", declared head of state Xi Jinping at his festive speech in Tiananmen Square in Beijing. No power can impede the progress of the Chinese people and nation. To substantiate the claim, he combined the seventieth anniversary celebration with the largest arms show in history to date.

The Chinese military made it clear that their military equipment is "completely self-produced", and that they do not rely on technological support from abroad. It was intended to demonstrate the "independent innovation capability" of the Chinese defence industry. Above all, "The Chinese military will resolutely defend national sovereignty, security and development interests".[65]

From G20 to G2 and back to G3

G20, G8, G7 – In fact, for some time now it has been boiling down to G2, the United States of America versus China. Both countries have been heading for a duel for some time – politically, economically and ultimately probably also in a military sense. For a long time after the collapse of the Soviet Union, the West no longer perceived Russia as a serious opponent. It was not until Moscow's brutal invasion of Ukraine in the spring of 2022 that it became unmistakably clear that the geopolitical power play is by no means determined by G2 alone but by G3: the USA, China and Russia. While the West's military confrontation with Russia has been obvious at least since the invasion of Ukraine, the signs of the potential for armed conflict with China are not quite so clear. But they do exist, as an incident in December 2018 showed.

Just before Christmas 2018, a US Navy destroyer, the Decatur, cruised in the South China Sea, a few miles from a reef that China claims as its territory and has developed into a weaponised base. All of a sudden, a guided missile destroyer of the Chinese Marine, the "Lanzhou", approached on a collision course. The Chinese announced "You are on a dangerous course. If you do not change course, you will have to suffer the consequences". The Americans replied "We are on peaceful passage". The two warships held their course, and the Chinese crew began to hang fenders over the rail to prepare their ship for a collision. With only about 45 yards left, the American captain conceded and swerved to starboard at the last minute. Had he stayed the course, fired or called the US Air Force to help, it could have been the beginning of the next world war. The Hong Kong-based "South China Morning Post", considered a reputable newspaper, wrote: "If the final stage of the geopolitical rivalry is military confrontation, the starting pistol may already have been fired". Because the near miss halfway between Vietnam and the Philippines was not an isolated incident – between 2016 and 2018 alone, the US Department of Defence reported a total of 18 "dangerous incidents". The evasion by the captain of the "Decatur" in December 2018 may have been a rational gesture, perhaps also the desire not to start World War III at Christmas time of all times but the evasive manoeuvre was not exemplary for either the geopolitical or military stance of the USA. "We will continue to fly, sail and operate wherever international law allows," clarified the then US Secretary of Defence James Mattis in light of the "Decatur" incident. And US Vice President Mike Pence already had "Air Force Two" fly 50 miles past the Spratley Islands, which are claimed by China, on its way to a conference in Singapore a month earlier. To this he commented: "Imperial behaviour and aggression have no place in the Indo-Pacific. We will not give in". China's leader Xi Jinping promptly countered that he would not give up "one inch" of Chinese territory. He ordered his officers to prepare "to wage war". To this end, he gave instructions to consider "all complex situations", to prepare "contingency plans" and to bolster the "combat readiness" of the troops. What he meant by this became abundantly clear three years later.

The Hague denies China's sovereignty in the region

On 12 July 2021, China's military said it "drove away" a US warship from waters near the Paracel Islands in the South China Sea on Monday. The destroyer "USS Benfold" had entered the area without permission. The USA had thus violated China's sovereignty and endangered stability in the South China Sea. "We urge the United States to immediately stop such provocative actions," a command of the Chinese armed forces announced.[66] The timing of the incident was probably no coincidence – 12 July 2021 marked the fifth anniversary of a ruling on China's territorial claims in the region. The Permanent Court of Arbitration in The Hague had ruled in 2016 that the People's Republic has no sovereign claims in the region. China claims more than 80 per cent of the three million square kilometre area for itself – even though some of the islands and reefs lie much closer to the coasts of other countries. The People's Republic justifies this with the so-called "nine-dash line", a mark on a map from the 1940s that extends far to the south. Beijing had already refused to accept the arbitration award in 2016 and declared the ruling "null and void".[67] Rich oil and gas deposits are believed to exist under the sea. It is also important for fishing. Chinese territorial claims are also a concern for other countries because important shipping routes run through the South China Sea. But far beyond these rational considerations, the USA in particular is undoubtedly concerned with making it clear to China and the international community that only one global power is entitled to do practically anything anywhere: the United States of America.

The People's Republic of China, the most populous country on earth with 1.4 billion people, and the Russian Federation, as

Russia is officially called, the largest country on earth by far with 17,000 million square kilometres, have a completely different perception of this.

The Thucydides Trap

When one superpower has caught up with another, war has often ensued in history. Harvard political scientist Graham Allison calls this constellation the "Thucydides trap", alluding to the great historian of ancient Greece. It ranges from the resistance of Sparta with the rising Athens to the clash of the British Empire and the German Empire before 1914.

Whether the trap between the USA as the world's number one power and the emerging China will snap shut is not necessarily a foregone conclusion. In contrast to earlier times, nowadays all world economies are so closely interconnected that any political confrontation, for example through sanctions or even military measures, inevitably leads to direct feedback at home. Moscow had to learn this painfully in view of the sanctions imposed by the West on the country after the invasion of Ukraine in 2022. The greatest danger for China was that it would also be caught up in the sanctions imposed by the West. It was certainly also the fear of this that kept Beijing from siding too obviously with Moscow after the Russian invasion of Ukraine.

But the extent to which China is preparing to take over world leadership from the USA was made clear by head of state Xi Jinping in his speech at the World Economic Forum 2021, which was held virtually because of the coronavirus pandemic. He presented himself as a global defender of law, freedom and democracy. While US President Joe Biden clearly evoked the danger of a cyber war in 2021: "I think that if we end up in a war – a real shooting war with a major power – it's going to be as a consequence of a cyber breach of great consequence. And the probability is increasing exponentially".[68] Xi Jinping declared "We should be committed to international law rather than seeking our own supremacy". This was a key phrase and a remarkable one coming from the Chinese leader. In ancient China, Xi Jinping said, "law was the true basis of governance". This also applies today and in world politics. Not the "law of the jungle" should determine relations between states but rules and consensus. The strong should not bully the weak," said President Xi Jinping. And further: "Decisions should not be made by simply showing off strong muscles or waving a big fist". The Charter of the United Nations is the basis of the international community, the Chinese leader declaimed at the World Economic Forum 2021. US President Biden was thus portrayed as a warmonger, while Xi positioned himself as a preserver of peace based on international law and an advocate of multilateralism.

This makes it clear: China is by no means prepared to be relegated to the "role of the villain" by the USA but wants its global expansion to be understood as a development consistent with international law. On the one hand, it is a rejection of the idea of "Cold War 2.0", and on the other hand, it is an attempt to attract as many states as possible, and especially Europe, to its side in precisely this bloc formation ("China versus the USA"), or at least to maintain a neutral stance between the parties.

But China's diplomatic subtlety is being disrupted by the brute force with which Russia has been trying to make itself heard in the world since 2022 at the latest.

The Russian worldview

Shortly after Russia's invasion of Ukraine in February 2022, the Russian news agency Ria inadvertently circulated a text falsely celebrating Russia's victory. Apparently, the editors had prepared the victory text in advance and published it prematurely by mistake. What was interesting about this was the historical context, the glimpse into the Russian soul.

Ria celebrated thus: "Russia's military operation in Ukraine has opened a new era". Russia is reinstating its unity," it said, referring to the Soviet Union, whose borders Putin has repeatedly described as "historic Russia". The "tragedy of 1991", of the break-up of the Soviet Union, had been "overcome. Yes, at a high price, yes, over tragic events of a de facto civil war, because now brothers are still shooting at each other," Ria wrote. "But Ukraine as anti-Russia will no longer exist," it said, applying a Putin quote that had often been applied among Moscow's elite.

According to this account, Russia "restored its historical fullness, gathered the Russian world, the Russian people together, in its totality of Great Russians, Belarusians and Little Russians", whereby the latter refers to the Ukrainians. Had Russia not done so but allowed "the temporary separation to solidify for centuries, we would not only have betrayed the memory of our ancestors but would also have been cursed by our descendants for allowing the Russian (sic) Earth to fall apart". Putin had assumed "historical responsibility" by deciding "not to leave the solution of the Ukrainian question to future generations". This was necessary so that Ukraine would not become "anti-Russia and an outpost of the West to pressurise us".

Bringing Ukraine "back to Russia" would have become "more difficult with each decade" due to a "recodification" and "derussification" of Ukrainians; Putin has also lamented this. According to Ria, if "the West had solidified total geopolitical and military control" over Ukraine, "its return to Russia would have become completely impossible – we would have had to fight the Atlantic bloc for it". But now, according to the victory commentary, "there is no such problem – Ukraine has returned to Russia". This does not mean that "its sovereignty will be dissolved" but that Ukraine will be "rebuilt, reinstated and brought back to its natural state as part of the Russian world".[69]

The commentary, written in the spirit of Putin, revealed the Russian point of view: Reinstating the historic Greater Russia is the most noble task, also to stop the steady advance of the West, the EU and NATO into Eastern Europe. It was perestroika and the associated disintegration of the Soviet Union that Putin and the national forces of Russia could not get over.

Perestroika and Glasnost

Perestroika, which translates as "rebuilding", "transformation", or "restructuring", refers to the process of modernising the Soviet Union's social, political and economic system initiated by Mikhail Gorbachev from the beginning of 1986. Gorbachev was General Secretary of the Central Committee of the

Communist Party of the Soviet Union (CPSU) from 1985 to August 1991 and President of the Soviet Union from March 1990 to December 1991. In addition to rebuilding, he also focused on "glasnost", i.e. openness, transparency, freedom of opinion and freedom of the press. Liberalisation, including facets of democratisation and the rollback of the planned economy, were the hallmarks of this era. In disarmament negotiations with the USA, Mikhail Gorbachev initiated the end of the Cold War and received the Nobel Peace Prize for it in 1990.

The reproach of subsequent Russian generations up to Putin was that Gorbachev had practically made a gift of the Soviet Union. While the Russians had disarmed and the Warsaw Pact, the Soviet Union's military alliance, had disintegrated, the West, with the EU and NATO, had, one might say, moved ever further east and crept dangerously close to Russia. It was this tone of behaviour that had not only fallen on Russia's ears but to some extent also on those of the Western world – at least before Russia launched its frontal attack on Ukraine.

Putin dreams of Great Russia

After the fall of the Soviet Union, Russia no longer played a significant role economically and politically at the end of the twentieth century. The memories of once glorious times weighed heavily on the land. When Vladimir Putin, a former officer of the Russian secret service, came to power, it was with the firm intention of reinstating the Russian bear's voice and respect in the world. Russia wanted to return to the world stage. Putin fought with words and weapons, in Syria, Eastern Europe and Africa. Time and again, he surprised the disunited West by striking tactical, brutal and opportunistic blows. Almost from the beginning, Vladimir Putin presented himself as a warlord who knew how to implement his moves on the chessboard of international politics with military force, in contravention of all the rules. Foreign policy became the raison d'être of his "Regency of Russia". For more than 20 years, the former lieutenant colonel worked on a new Greater Russia – an ambitious goal that he pursued resolutely.

After the West, under US leadership, had defeated the Soviet Union, the political approach of the United States of America in particular was characterised by an almost conspicuously arrogant certainty of victory. Communism had been defeated, Russia had been reduced to a seemingly insignificant second-rate power, China had not yet emerged as a new enemy and the global supremacy of the USA seemed unchallenged. During this time, NATO advanced steadily in the direction of Russia: Poland, Hungary, the Czech Republic, Romania, Bulgaria and also the Baltic states gradually joined the Western alliance. It was probably these years that nurtured the desire in Russia as well as in China to counter the overpowering USA with a position of power of their own.

In February 2007, Vladimir Putin fired the first warning shot. In an appearance at the Munich Conference on Security Policy from 9 to 11 February, he denounced the USA's blatant quest for exclusive world supremacy in a speech marked by rancour and fury. In his Munich speech in 2007, Putin drew a red line for the first time, for which any trespassing by the West would inevitably trigger a backlash. Anyone who was surprised by Russia's attack on Ukraine in 2022 had not been listening in Munich in 2007. At that time, Putin clearly proclaimed Russia's return to the world stage – with the claim of an independent power on an equal footing with the West. The USA was not prepared for Russia's resurgence; instead of taking Putin's words seriously and taking them into account in their policy, they labelled the man in the Kremlin as the harbinger of a new Cold War. Putin, who before 2007 had by all means attempted a rapprochement with Western Europe, became Europe's bogeyman – comparable to Turkish President Recep Erdoğan but equipped with considerably more military power. But since 2007 there has been only one goal for Vladimir Putin: to put Russia back on the world stage.

NATO, not taking Putin's warning seriously, continued its eastward expansion to Russia's borders in 2008. The West simply ignored the Kremlin's doctrine – "hands off our immediate neighbours". On the contrary, the West began to discuss the possible admission of Georgia and Ukraine to NATO. Alarm bells chimed in Russia. It was no coincidence that at the same time in the Russian-speaking regions of Abkhazia and South Ossetia in Georgia, the simmering conflicts there flared up again. In the wake of the collapse of the Soviet Union, Georgia had become an independent state in 1991. But in the regions of Abkhazia and South Ossetia, the aim from the beginning was to break away from Georgia. Georgia initially believed it had the situation under control. But on August 7, 2008, Russian tanks rolled into the country. Apparently, Russia saw the local autonomy efforts as an opportunity and helped both regions achieve some form of independence in a blitzkrieg that lasted from August 7 to August 15, 2008. For the first time since the end of the Soviet Union, the Russian bear had left its den again. Georgia lost about 20 percent of its territory.

Since then, the "Republic of Abkhazia" has called itself an independent state but most countries in the world consider it part of Georgia. Nevertheless, Abkhazia has had independent state structures from Georgia since 1993 and Georgia does not exercise any sovereignty over the territory.[70] Similarly in South Ossetia: The region south of the Caucasus Mountains belongs to Georgia under international law but is de facto independent and internationally recognized by five states, of which only Russia and Syria are of concern. There are two other disputed regions, Arzakh and Transnistria, which together with Abkhazia and South Ossetia form a community of unrecognised states and support each other's sovereignty aspirations.[71]

In much of the West, these connections are little known. Only the 2008 five-day war in the South Caucasus between Georgia on the one hand and Russia and the Russian-backed regions of South Ossetia and Abkhazia on the other received brief attention in the Western media. In the process, approximately 850 people were killed and between 2500 and 3000 people were wounded.[72]

The 2008 Georgia crisis and the 2022 Ukraine war both followed one and the same pattern: Russia supported the pro-Russian groups there in order to take de facto power in the end. In both cases, Russia intervened after it became clear that the countries directly on its border would join the EU and NATO, respectively.

In both cases, the political message was unambiguous, albeit twofold. First of all, when Russian security concerns are directly involved, Russia does not shy away from the military option. Secondly, the new allies targeted by Georgia or Ukraine, i.e. the EU or NATO, will not intervene militarily, in order to avoid a major war with Russia. This message was already clear in Georgia in 2008 but it obviously did not prevent Ukraine from also reaching out to the West – until history repeated itself. The West supplied war material, took in the refugees and imposed quite harsh sanctions against Russia but explicitly avoided military intervention.

The struggle for Ukraine began in 2004

The war in Ukraine entered 2019 with a headlong escalation but it had begun long before in 2004, when the then Ukrainian President Viktor Yushchenko declared that his country aspired to early membership in the European Union. On 9 September 2008, Ukraine and the EU did indeed reach an accord on an Association Agreement.[73]

The European Commission announced: "The EU is committed to an increasingly close partnership with Ukraine, aiming at gradual economic integration and deepening political cooperation".[74]

The announcement by the Ukrainian government in November 2013 that it would not sign the Association Agreement with the European Union for the time being was even more surprising. Under pressure from Moscow, then Ukrainian President Viktor Yanukovych refused to sign the agreement with the EU. In doing so, however, he incurred the wrath of the population that wanted to turn their backs on Russia and embrace the West. The uprising began on Independence Square (Maidan Nesaleshnosti).[75] In the course of the so-called Euromaidan, hundreds of thousands of Ukrainians took to the streets. Despite strong state repression, it took the state weeks to suppress the protests. After the agreed settlement of the conflict through a treaty brokered by the foreign ministers of Germany, France and Poland on February 21, 2014, Yanukovych fled the scene hastily that same night, whereupon the parliament rejected him on 22 February The Euromaidan came to an end with the appointment of Oleksandr Turchynov as interim president on 23 February and finally with the formation of an interim government under Arseniy Yatsenyuk on 26 February, after the head of government, Azarov, and the entire government had already left on 28 January in order to forestall his planned deposition. During the final phase, the Russian annexation of Crimea and the destabilisation of the country through Russia's armed incursion into eastern Ukraine began.

In this situation, the Russian government apparently saw its chance to stop Ukraine's rapprochement with the European Union and to annexe at least parts of the country, especially the eastern Ukrainian areas ("oblasts") of Donetsk and Luhansk. In both areas, pro-Russian forces began to work towards secession. It remained unclear to what extent exactly the Russian government fomented the emerging unrest but it was clear that Russian-backed militias, regular Russian and Ukrainian troops and volunteer militias participated in the fighting. To all appearances, the military conflict did not start with the inhabitants but with the armed units. In this respect, one cannot speak of a civil war. Russia played a downright deadly farce when state media announced that Russian soldiers had voluntarily travelled to the combat zone – some even as tourists – and died on the spot as "heroes". Several paratroopers had landed in Ukraine by mistake, Russian information policy just coquetted with the world.[76] The Ukrainian government declared some 4,000 pro-Russian fighters to be terrorists.[77]

But Russia fought back militarily, and diplomatically as well. Thus, on 15 April 2014, Russian President Vladimir Putin demanded in a telephone conversation with UN Secretary-General Ban Ki-moon that the United Nations" condemn the unconstitutional actions of the leaders in Kyiv". Ukraine had already appealed to the UN and called for the deployment of Blue Helmets. Ban Ki-moon rejected this with the words "We cannot launch an operation without a clear mandate from the Security Council". At the same time, it had long been clear to the UN Secretary-General that, in view of Russia's veto, the Security Council would never agree to a mandate in Ukraine. The United Nations was – once again – caught in the veto trap.

After all, in June 2014, i.e. a brief time later, the United Nations complained of massive human rights violations in the parts of Ukraine attacked by Russia. [78] A month later, the UN declared a total breakdown of law and order and spoke of a reign of terror by armed groups over the population with deprivations of freedom, kidnappings, torture and executions.[79]

UN appeals to the OSCE remain futile

Nevertheless, the UN avoided direct interference beyond observation and comment and escalated the conflict to the Organisation for Security and Co-operation in Europe (OSCE), a permanent peacekeeping conference of states affiliated to it under Chapter VIII of the UN Charter. As the name suggests, the OSCE is primarily responsible for Europe – and thus certainly for the Ukraine conflict – but the fifty-seven participating states, including all European countries and Turkey and all successor states of the Soviet Union, also include the USA and Canada. In this way, the OSCE in a way mirrors the fronts of the Cold War, and the conflict in Ukraine indeed turned out to be a kind of revival of the Cold War that had probably been long thought forgotten.

The OSCE failed completely to defuse the military conflict. Even in the period of a fragile ceasefire – the so-called "Minsk I Protocol" – that started in September 2014, which the OSCE monitored, 1,300 combatants and civilians died within four months.[80] Even after a renewed Ceasefire Agreement in February 2015 – Minsk II – the fighting did not stop but continued year after year.

In 2017 alone, the OSCE registered over 400,000 (!) violations of the ceasefire. It is like a Swiss cheese with so many holes that you cannot see any cheese at all. The OSCE had over seven hundred observers on duty, who prepared a report day after day, recording every little detail of the change.[81] In view of the extremely confusing situation, this was a mammoth bureaucratic task but it did not bring one iota of relief to the people in the strife-torn regions.

It was obvious from the beginning that the infiltration of Ukraine by Russian troops was part of Russia's plan to regain, at least in small parts, its territory that had shrunk with the end of the Soviet Union. As early as February 2014, a strategy paper circulated that described Russia's possible behaviour towards Ukraine in seven points.[82] Shortly afterwards, the first troops without national emblems invaded the peninsula. They were obviously Russian troops, as Russian President Vladimir Putin admitted on Russian state television about a year later. On 18 March 2014,Crimea was officially annexed by Russia.[83]

Crimea: Part of Russia since Catherine the Great

From the Russian perspective, the state had only appropriated what had always belonged to it. After all, the Crimea had already been declared Russian "henceforth and for all time" on 8 April 1783 by the Russian Empress Catherine II – also known as "Catherine the Great "– who played a similar hand when she dissociated the peninsula from the Ottoman Empire in the Russo-Turkish War of 1768-1774. Since the annexation in 2014, Crimea has de facto belonged to Russia again, although the international community continued to classify Crimea as an autonomous republic within Ukrainian territory. This was also the attitude of the United Nations when it urged the preservation of the territorial integrity of Ukraine within its internationally recognised borders in UN General Assembly Resolution A/RES/68/262 entitled "Territorial Integrity of Ukraine".

In the UN Security Council, a resolution to this effect was initially rejected by Russia, so the General Assembly took up the issue.[84] The resolution had no impact; only the Security Council could have decided to deploy Blue Helmets. But there was no mandate for that, nor would the deployment of UN-troops against the Russian military – that could have triggered the Third World War – have been a conceivable option even for a moment.

Home of the Black Sea Fleet

A look at the Ukrainian port city of Sevastopol, which lies on the Crimea, shows why Russia was so vehement about losing the Crimean Peninsula to the West. Sevastopol was Russia's only access to the southern waters during the Soviet period and was therefore of vital interest to Moscow. Russian ships can reach the Russian base at Tartus on the eastern Mediterranean coast in Syria from the Black Sea via the Turkish Strait. So, for Moscow, Sevastopol is like a steppingstone into the Mediterranean. For Russia, it is therefore a nightmare that Sevastopol could one day be a NATO base if Ukraine were to put its planned accession to NATO into practice.[85]

The fact that Sevastopol belonged to Ukraine is in any case due to a curious coincidence of history. In 1954, the then General Secretary of the Communist Party, Nikita Khrushchev, transferred the Crimean Peninsula from Russian hands to the Ukrainian Soviet Republic – together with the port city of Sevastopol, the scene of countless Russian legends from the Crimean War to the siege by the German Wehrmacht and the seat of the much-praised Black Sea Fleet. As long as the Soviet Union existed, the donation was only a political gesture without consequences. But when the Soviet Union collapsed in 1991, Crimea and Sevastopol were assigned to Ukraine and thus became a bone of contention.

After Ukrainian President Yanukovych fled Kyiv on 22 February 2014 under pressure from the Maidan protests, supporters and opponents of a transfer of power took to the streets on the Ukrainian peninsula of Crimea. In the morning hours of 27 February 2014 armed forces occupied strategically important points in Crimea. The soldiers without rank and nationality insignia on their uniforms – derided by the Ukrainian public as "little green men" – were apparently Russian special forces. They soon controlled the regional parliament and the regional government building in the capital Simferopol – and hoisted the Russian flag on official buildings. The regional parliament, occupied by the armed forces, elected the politician Sergey Aksyonov of the "Russian Unity" party as the new head of government in camera – without the consent of the Ukrainian president, as stipulated in the Ukrainian constitution. On 6 March 2014, the newly established regional parliament decided to annex Crimea to the Russian Federation. At the same time, a referendum was scheduled for 16 March in which the majority Russian-speaking population was to decide on the future status of Crimea. More than 95 per cent of the voters are said to have opted for Russia, with international observers considering both the legality of the referendum and the vote illegitimate. On 18 March 2014, Vladimir Putin signed a treaty on the incorporation of Crimea into the Russian Federation. Since then, Moscow considers the Crimean Peninsula, including Sevastopol, to be part of Russia.[86]

The annexation of Crimea was undoubtedly a great victory for Putin and was celebrated as such in Moscow. It also marked the start of a kind of patriotic spring in Moscow, the beginning of a new era of "make Russia great again". Vladimir Putin saw himself in the historic role of the one who holds the Soviet states together and restores Russia's honour. Around the same time, and fuelled by Moscow, conflicts began in the Russian-speaking Donbass region, also called the Donetsk Basin, in eastern Ukraine. Later, the eastern regions in the Donbass, Donetsk and Luhansk, were recognised by Russia as independent "people's republics".[87] As it happened after the annexation of Crimea, Moscow earned international criticism for its actions – but nothing more happened.

Russia seizes Syria

While the West was still fuming over the takeover of Crimea, Putin was apparently already planning his next move – in Syria. Under the guise of counterterrorism, the war in Syria had long since become confusing by this time. Islamist militias, the Free Syrian Army, the Kurdish militia and the troops of Syria's President Bashar Hafiz al-Assad fought each other. Western diplomacy during this period was characterised by moralising and hesitation.

In hardly any conflict has the impotence of the international community of states been so striking as in Syria since 2011.

The war in Syria is a never-ending carnage in which more than 400,000 people have been killed and over a million injured, maimed and crippled since 2011. More than eleven million fled, many of them bound for Europe, where they contributed significantly to the so-called "second refugee crisis".

The United Nations repeatedly tried to end this bloodbath in Syria. But all efforts have been in vain.

Four decades of Assad

For over four decades, the family of President Al-Assad has ruled Syria, one of the most repressive countries in the Arab world. Bashar Al-Assad succeeded his father in 2000. When protests against the governments were voiced in several Arab states in December 2010 and the so-called "Arab Spring" took its course, resistance against the president also began to stir in Syria. While the revolutions in Tunisia, in several states in the Middle East and in North Africa led to changes, the Syrian president has resisted all attempts to hound him out of office from the beginning and even now, on the publication of this book. In the process, he has consistently applied force against the demonstrators. School children who wrote the phrase "The people want the overthrow of the regime" on walls in March 2011 were arrested and tortured by the security forces. On 18 March, the regime applied force against peaceful demonstrators demanding the release of the children and democratisation of the country, claiming that "armed gangs and terrorists" were to blame for the escalation. Calls for Al-Assad to step down went unheard.

The wave of initially largely peaceful protests and violent repression quickly engulfed several Syrian cities, including the major cities of Hama and Homs, as well as the capital, Damascus, and its outskirts. At times the regime lost control but it did not collapse; instead, it launched a counterattack. This marked the beginning of Syria's long journey to the edge of the abyss, one could also say, into the abyss. Political calls for reform even from Syria's allies such as Russia and Iran went unheard. Apparently, the Assad regime was afraid to engage in a reform process at the end of which accountability could be demanded – as happened in Egypt and Tunisia, for example. The involvement of large parts of the country's political elite in the massive human rights violations of 2011 alone made it unlikely that Al-Assad and his henchmen would get off lightly in such a trial.[88]

The UN Plan for Syria

Against this background, the United Nations appointed its former Secretary-General Kofi Annan as Special Envoy for Syria in

February 2012. With a 6-point plan, he wanted to achieve a ceasefire by April 2012 and thus create the basis for a UN observer mission in Syria.[89] To this end, the UN Security Council adopted Resolution 2043 on 21 April 2012, which authorised this observer mission.[90] It was the first measure in a long series of negotiations and declarations, all of which were marked by failure. After only a few weeks, the UN had to vacate its observation post because even for military observers the situation had become too dangerous.

But of course, the country remained under surveillance and about a year later it was discovered that there had been poison gas attacks against the population in the Ghouta region east of Damascus on 21 August 2013. The UN concluded that surface-to-surface missiles had been fired with the chemical warfare agent Sarin in a highly concentrated form.[91] The number of fatalities varied between 281 and 1729, depending on the source.[92] Thousands of people were admitted to hospitals with neurotoxic reactions. The Assad regime was suspected of being the aggressor because the Sarin gas came from the stocks of the Syrian army but this reference could never be corroborated.[93]

It could thus never be ruled out that another civil war party was responsible for the gas atrocities. It should not be overlooked that the battle line in Syria did not run in a linear fashion between "the rebels" and "the regime" but that many of the rebel groups were enemies of each other and that, accordingly, the principle of "everyone against everyone" had been adopted. Thus, in addition to the regular troops, mainly Shiite militias, such as the Lebanese Hezbollah, fought on the side of the government, because Assad belonged to the Shiite Alewites sect. These in turn received support from Iran, which fought a kind of proxy war against Saudi Arabia on Syrian soil.

Therefore, various Sunni groups fought against the Assad regime with Saudi support. Sunnis make up most of the population in Syria with moderate as well as radical rebels. As if that were not enough, the terrorist organisation "Islamic State" (IS) also took advantage of the chaos of the civil war to invade large parts of Syria. The terrorist militia that emerged in Iraq had set out with the aim of establishing an Arab caliphate. The IS fighters made a name for themselves with torture and mass murders.

This regime of horror was opposed by an "International Alliance against the Islamic State" led by the USA. The United States founded this military alliance on 5 September 2014 at the NATO summit together with the United Kingdom, France, Italy, Germany, Poland, Denmark, Australia, Canada and Turkey.[94] Later, the Netherlands (October 2014 to July 2016) and Belgium joined. The latter since June 2016.[95] According to the US President in office at the time, Barack Obama, more than sixty countries participated in the war against IS, although not all of them militarily.

Putin seized the opportunity to support al-Assad. A totalitarian regime sealing off his country was far better for Putin than the prevailing chaos, the possible takeover by the Islamists or even US successes in this region of the world.

From 2011, the so-called Arab Spring spread like wildfire – from Tunisia to Libya and Egypt to Syria. Putin apparently suspected that the USA was behind this development and obviously feared that the resulting power vacuum would favour the spread of radical Islam. To counteract this development, Moscow intervened with a military operation in Syria on 30 September 2015. It was Russia's first military deployment outside its neighbouring countries. The attacks, also on civilian targets, were mainly conducted from the air. On the ground, Putin used foreign mercenaries so as not to have to explain dead Russian soldiers in Moscow. Experts speak of so-called hybrid warfare, which was also deployed in eastern Ukraine. This is how Putin managed to keep Bashar al-Assad in power – completely surprising for the West, which had already written him off. After all, the former leaders Ben Ali in Tunisia,[96] Muammar al-Gaddafi in Libya[97] and Hosni Mubarak in Egypt[98] were swept away by the Arab Spring. But al-Assad stayed, thanks to Moscow's military help. Since then, Russia has vigorously expanded the port of Tartus and the air base in Hmeimin to consolidate its presence in the Mediterranean.

Meanwhile, Russia scored not only a military victory in Syria but also a power-political one – after the UN had failed for years.

On 24 February 2018, the United Nations Security Council unanimously adopted Resolution 2401 on the situation in Syria at its 8188th meeting. In it, the UN's most powerful organ demanded a ceasefire from all parties to the conflict for at least 30 days. The fleeting period of peace was intended to allow humanitarian organisations access to the heavily contested areas to care for war victims and bring them to safety. The UN High Commissioner for Human Rights, Seid Ra'ad al-Hussein warned that the nearly 400,000 desperate and starving children, women and men in the rebel area of Eastern Ghouta were facing an "apocalypse". During the ceasefire, volunteers were to deliver enough food and medicine to the starving population with their convoys, as well as evacuate the wounded and sick. The brief time without fighting was supposed to benefit primarily the people in the vicinity of Eastern Ghouta.

The UN Security Council struggled for a long time over the wording of the resolution, which was supposed to bring the desired ceasefire at least temporarily. Russia managed to have the bombardment of jihadist groups in Syria such as "Islamic State" and Al-Qaeda as well as "other individuals, groups, units with links to Al-Qaeda and IS" excluded from the ceasefire in the resolution text. So shooting was still allowed but more selectively than before. Thus, the resolution was meaningless from the beginning because Syria's Bashar al-Assad classified all rebels per se as terrorists, even those explicitly supported by the West.

Thus, the United Nations document proved not to be worth the paper it was printed on. Indeed, the regime of Bashar al-Assad continued to sow the seeds of bloodshed during the ceasefire called in Eastern Ghouta. There was no question of "all parties ceasing hostilities," as the UN paper put it.

A total of ten Syria resolutions failed in the United Nations Security Council due to Russia's veto. The deployment of military observers, ceasefires or sanctions because of poison gas attacks – Russia obstructed everything. And the content of those resolutions issued by the Security Council was so downplayed that they had no effect.

Moscow, on the other hand, had become a player on the world stage again with its unexpected intervention in Syria. Shiites as well as Sunnis, i.e. the two largest religious currents of Islam, were grateful to Putin for repelling the terrorist organisation Islamic State (IS). Whether in Iran, Saudi Arabia, Israel or Turkey – Vladimir Putin was welcomed everywhere after his intervention in Syria.

Private mercenaries on the rise

When states do not want to deploy soldiers, they deploy private mercenaries. Most of the time, this is done covertly but Russian President Vladimir Putin already made it clear in 2019 that he sees nothing reprehensible in this. However, he chose to circumvent the issue: it was perfectly legitimate for the Putin confidant and oligarch Yevgeny Prigozhin to hire the so-called Wagner Group – a mercenary group – to enforce his interests anywhere in the world – but only if he did not violate Russian law. Putin said: "I repeat, they are not breaking Russian laws and have the right to work anywhere in the world and defend their business interests. If the Wagner Group disregards any laws, the public prosecutor's office will have to make a legal assessment." This indirectly confirms the assumption that the Kremlin had also deployed the mercenaries in the Syrian civil war. However, Putin has never admitted this.[99]

Russia's charm offensive in Africa

Strengthened by his successes in Syria, Putin turned his gaze towards the Mediterranean, especially Libya, which is a desert state but has plenty of oil. He apparently once again saw a favourable opportunity to exploit the weaknesses of the USA and the United Nations, which in his estimation were responsible for the chaos in Libya.

On 19 March 2019, French, British and American aircraft had attacked the troops of the Libyan autocrat Gaddafi. Their declared goal: to save the civilian population. The West still believed that it could make peace there and introduce democracy. But after the fall of Gaddafi, the country descended into chaos.

As in Syria, Turks and Russians fought each other in Libya. The two powers divided up the oil-rich country, which is also a gateway to Africa and ensures presence in the Mediterranean, like a cake. For Russia, this was by no means restricted to the sea area commonly referred to as the Mediterranean but also included the navigable connections between the Red Sea, the Black Sea, the Mediterranean and access to the Atlantic via Gibraltar.

In the armed conflict between troops and militias of the government of Fayiz as-Saraj under the *Government of National Accord* (GNA), which controls parts of western Libya with the capital Tripoli, and the troops of the ruler of eastern Libya, Khalifa Haftar, Putin backed the latter and received Khalifa Haftar with full honours on a Russian aircraft carrier on 11 January 2015. On 7 November 2018, Haftar apparently met the head of the Wagner mercenary group in Moscow, which had already done the "groundwork" for Putin's invasion in Syria. In Libya, around 2,000 "ghost soldiers" of the Wagner troop landed shortly afterwards to serve Haftar. The Kremlin categorically stated that there were no Russian soldiers on Libyan operational territory. In this way, Russia had secured access to the largest oil reserves in Africa. Putin reached an agreement with Turkish leader Recep Erdoğan on the division of Libya. The failure of the West had – once again – helped Russia to win. Putin and Erdoğan are quite similar in that both despots rule without regard for Western sensitivities such as democracy or human rights. This does not make them friends but partners if it suits their own power strategy – even though Ankara, as a NATO partner strongly supported the West in its attempt to drive Russia out of Ukraine in 2022. This could well be a model for how China and Russia deal with each other – not as friends but as partners who are mutually beneficial as far as it suits their own strategy.

After victories in Syria and Libya, Vladimir Putin launched a broad-based "charm offensive" towards Africa in October 2019. An Africa Summit in Sochi was attended by the heads of state and government of almost all African states: 45 heads of state from 54 countries. The "deal" was obvious: Moscow would supply the despots with weapons, and the African countries would in turn provide the abundant raw materials of the black continent for Russian companies. Moreover, the African states would give Russia their voice at the United Nations wherever possible. Thirty African countries signed a military agreement with the Kremlin. The US was no longer seen as dependable and China was increasingly regarded as a threat; so Russia was the perfect new partner. Unlike the West, Moscow did not try to teach the Africans lessons in democracy and human rights but managed the deal as a sober business transaction. In January 2018, the first large arms shipment from Russia arrived in the Central African Republic – as a symbol of Russia arming Africa.

Putin's world history as a children's film

How good Vladimir Putin is at putting his own spin on world history and, above all, presenting it to the public, was featured at the time in a children's film. In it, the animals of Africa, lions, giraffes and elephants, were threatened by greedy hyenas – until the strong bear rushed in from Russia to free and protect Africa. The hyenas symbolised the West, or more precisely, the French as the former colonial power of Central Africa. It was a simple narrative but it worked on children and adults alike, especially since the Russians actually invested in local schools and hospitals, something the French had neglected for decades. The money for this came from the exploitation of raw materials. It was like a "perfect deal" for Russia's power politics and the well-being of the domestic population.

Operation "Iron Fist"

Far away from Africa, people in Moscow were worried in the meantime because Turkish President Recep Erdoğan was tampering with the borders of the "Russian empire". In 2020, for example, Turkey began to forge ahead with the conquest of the Armenian mountain of Karabakh with the help of Azerbaijan. Putin stopped the Turkish advance and thus sealed Russia's return to the Caucasus, even if he had to sacrifice Armenia as an ally to do so. On 27 September 2020, Azerbaijan launched the military operation "Iron Fist". Turkey supported the oil-rich Azerbaijan, and after 25 days Armenia had to capitulate. Then Russia ended the cruel power game: on 10 November 2020, direct hostilities ended in a Russian-brokered Ceasefire Agreement between the parties to the conflict. The Kremlin once again presented itself as a peacemaker and at the same time had regained control of the South Caucasus, which had been lost with the end of the Soviet Union. Moreover, the Turkish influence, which had long been a thorn in Putin's side, was ousted.

On 9 May 2021, Vladimir Putin celebrated peace with great pomp on Red Square in Moscow – at least officially. In reality, it was a victory celebration on the occasion of Russia's successful return to the world stage of international politics. The world began to fear Vladimir Putin again. Kremlin observers claim that even as a young boy he always wanted to play the leader on the farm. He has obviously taken this trait with him into world politics.

One must consider these overwhelming successes from the Russian point of view if one wants to understand why Putin launched an invasion of Ukraine in 2022. In this context, the role of Belarus must also be considered, at least in passing: On 24 February 2022, Russian troops also attacked Ukraine from Belarus. President Alexander Lukashenko, who has been in power since 1994 and who was confirmed in office in a dubious presidential election in 2020, has long been considered a friend of Putin. After Lukashenko had a passenger plane of the Irish airline Ryanair intercepted on 23 May 2021 in order to arrest an opposition member who was on the plane, the EU imposed sanctions on him. This has apparently driven him even closer to Russia, making Belarus a state subject to Vladimir Putin's influence.

But it was not until February 2022 that Russia's years of power struggles first erupted into a war in Europe. On the night of the 23rd to the 24th, the Russian military launched a major attack on Ukraine.

The Russian invasion of Ukraine

The Ukrainian capital Kyiv is about 750 kilometres flight-line distance from Moscow. The goal of the Russian invasion, which began on 24 February 2022, was apparently intended from the outset to capture Kyiv, overthrow the Ukrainian government and bring the country completely under Russian control – as quickly and as silently as possible. At the same time, Russian President Vladimir Putin also went out of his way to downplay the war from the very beginning. He described it as a "special military operation" necessary to pacify a Western-initiated escalation in eastern Ukraine.

Putin's propaganda machine was initially quite successful in establishing this narrative among his own population. On the day the war began, the Russian polling institute Levada published a survey according to which 60 per cent of the population classified the USA and the countries of NATO as aggressors in eastern Ukraine.[100] Putin spoke of a "foreign deployment" of his soldiers and announced in a televised speech: "I have decided to carry out a special military operation". He was responding to a "written request from the heads of the Luhansk and Donetsk People's Republics for assistance in repelling attacks by the Ukrainian army".

He reasoned: "The aim is to protect the people who have been subjected to bullying and genocide for the last eight years. And for this we will strive for the demilitarisation and denazification of Ukraine." At the same time, he called on the Ukrainian army to immediately lay down its arms.[101] It was a ridiculous justification for the world, suitable at best for dissemination via the state media as a justification to the Russian population.

While Putin stunned everyone with his flat-out lie, Ukrainian President Volodymyr Zelenskyy earned international recognition for his courage. The former comedian was elected president in April 2019 with around 73 per cent. After a night of thunderous bombardment in Kyiv, he posted a 40-second selfie video on 26 February 2022 with a clear message: "I am here. We will not lay down our arms. We will defend our state."

By this time, according to Putin's will, Zelenskyy should have long since absconded, been killed or captured. Indeed, eliminating Volodymyr Zelenskyy as quickly as possible was one of the main objectives of Putin's military machine in the attack on Kyiv.[102]

After initial hesitation, Germany abandoned its principle of not supplying weapons to crisis areas in the face of the Russians' ruthless advance. On 26 February 2022, the German government authorised the Netherlands to deliver 400 German-made RPGs (anti-tank weapons) to Ukraine to support the war against Russian aggressors. In addition, 500 "Stinger" surface-to-air missiles from stocks of the German Armed Forces were delivered to Ukraine.[103] In addition, there were 14 armoured vehicles and up to 10,000 tonnes of fuel exported to Ukraine via Poland.[104]

Germany's decision, almost a U-turn, hinged on the fact that the Russian Ministry of Defence had threatened to "extend the advance in all directions" after Ukraine had refused to negotiate a ceasefire, according to the Russians. Ukraine, on the other hand, stressed that it was open to such negotiations but not under ultimatums or unreasonable conditions. At that time, Ukraine had already suffered around 200 war deaths and more than a thousand injuries.[105] In the course of 27 February, both sides agreed to start peace negotiations.[106]

By this time, Germany had long since clearly sided with Ukraine. Chancellor Olaf Scholz announced in the German Bundestag addressed to Ukraine: "As democrats, as Europeans, we stand by their side – on the right side of history". The actions of Russian President Vladimir Putin are inhumane, in breach of international law and "There is nothing and nobody that can justify it". "The appalling injustice, the pain of the Ukrainian people – they affect us all very deeply," said Scholz. Russia's President Vladimir Putin had "cold-bloodedly launched a war of aggression". Scholz described this as a "watershed in the history of our continent". "The world thereafter will no longer be the same as before. At the heart of the matter is the question of whether force can be allowed to break the law and whether Putin can be allowed to turn back the clocks to the heyday of the superpowers of the nineteenth century. Or whether we have it in us to keep warmongers like Putin in check". The Russian president has created a new reality that requires an unequivocal response, Scholz said on 27 February 2022.

The Ukrainian Ambassador in Berlin, Andrij Melnyk, expressed his gratitude effusively on behalf of his country: "We are glad that Germany finally made this 180-degree turnaround. I have always told my German friends and the federal government that they will not be able to endure the terrible images of the war in Ukraine for long without reacting and changing course. The Germans have finally woken up and started to act properly".[107] Before the end of February 2022, German Chancellor Olaf Scholz declared the German government's change of course regarding arms deliveries: "The Russian invasion of Ukraine marks a turning point. It threatens our entire post-war order. In this situation, it is our duty to do our utmost to support Ukraine in its defence against Vladimir Putin's invading army. Germany stands closely with Ukraine".[108]

Germany soft-pedals with Russia and China

That was a turning point for Germany. Before that, German politics had been soft-pedalling with Vladimir Putin for a good 15 years. No other country has forgiven him as much as the Federal Republic. When Moscow waged war in Georgia in autumn 2008, the German political and business elite gathered at the Russian embassy in Berlin for a lavish party with caviar, champagne and music. From the invasion of Georgia to the annexation of Crimea – Germany has always found a way to forgive its friend in the East. The reasoning goes that exclusion would not help anyone. Critics called this "a German reflex to avoid confrontation through dialogue." Even after Putin annexed Crimea and triggered the war in eastern Ukraine, Berlin was unwilling to join the US in imposing sanctions on Moscow.[109]

No one stands for Germany's kid-glove treatment of Moscow as symbolically as former Chancellor Gerhard Schröder. Schröder had already worked closely with Putin during his chancellorship from 1998 to 2005. He never made a secret of this. After the end of his political career, the former chancellor became Putin's most important lobbyist: seven years after his term in office, he accepted a directorial position at the Russian state corporation Gazprom. In 2017, he joined the management team of another Russian energy giant: Rosneft. The EU put the company on its sanctions list after Russia's invasion of Ukraine in spring 2022. But it was probably not only a question of a lot of money but also of friendship.

Schröder invited Putin to Hanover for his 60th birthday. The former chancellor celebrated his 70th birthday with Putin in St. Petersburg.[110] Shortly before, Russia had annexed the Black Sea peninsula of Crimea, which belongs to Ukraine under international law.

Incidentally, the German policy of understanding for the other side, as it was demonstrated to Moscow, can be similarly applied to Beijing. While Russia lured primarily by the supposedly secure energy supply and the desire for a "good neighbourly relationship", China attracted primarily by the enormous profits and by the prospect of benefiting the German economy. In 2020, China was Germany's largest trading partner for the fifth year in a row.[111] An example: In the first half of 2021, the People's Republic of China accounted for around 41 percent (!) of the global sales of Germany's largest automotive group, Volkswagen.[112] The comparison between Germany's soft-pedalling with Russia and kid-glove treatment of China is therefore not far-fetched – until the "rude awakening" comes, as in the case of Russia in 2022.

Germany's closeness to Russia, exemplified by Gerhard Schröder, is likely to have played a significant role in Europe's longstanding perception of Russia as a friend rather than a foe. However, this could also have led Putin, conversely, not to take the West seriously enough.

The Ukrainian-Western offensive

Vladimir Putin had apparently underestimated the combative spirit of the Ukrainians and the Western world. The invasion in the spring of 2022 was seen with remarkable unanimity as a general attack on the West, i.e. Western democracies, and the sanctity of the sovereignty of the borders of independent states.

How seriously the West took the matter was evident from the fact that only two days after the invasion, the Western states decided to exclude Russian banks from the international payment system Swift.[113] Founded in 1973 and based in Belgium, the Society for Worldwide Interbank Financial Telecommunication (Swift) operates a particularly secure telecommunications network (the SWIFTNet) that is used by more than 11,000 banks around the globe to transmit international payment instructions. In other words: Anyone who is excluded from the Swift system is completely cut off from international payment transactions. The exclusion of Russian banks represented a general attack by the West on Russian finance. This move was easily possible because Swift is legally a cooperative owned by the banks and based in Belgium, subject to the legal system of the European Union.[114] It was one of the most severe sanctions imposed by the West, partly because it prevented Russia from making payments to or receiving payments from the West. The supply of Russian gas to Europe and especially to Germany was thus directly endangered; why should Russia still send gas through the pipelines to the West if payment for it was no longer possible at all. Conversely, Western companies doing business in Russia could no longer receive cash flows from Putin's country overnight. In other words, not only Russia suffered from the Swift sanctions but also the Western economy and ultimately the supply situation in Western Europe. It was therefore a particularly clear signal of unity from the Western world to put Putin in his place.

EU Commission President Ursula von der Leyen summed up the reasoning: "We want to prevent Putin from using his state reserves to finance his war". Therefore, the assets of the Russian Central Bank have also been blocked. Moreover, the access of numerous Russian oligarchs to their financial assets has been restricted.[115] The Russian currency, the rouble, promptly plunged to a record low .[116]

Not only did the international community oppose Putin's expansion plans, but hackers also fought on the side of the West. Hackers are "actually" considered criminals who invade other people's computers and manipulate or destroy data, steal cryptocurrencies or extort ransom money. Not so at the beginning of the Ukraine crisis in February 2022. The international hacker collective Anonymous declared "cyber war" on the day of the invasion of Vladimir Putin's government and immediately set to work. Just over half an hour after their declaration of war, the hackers took over the website of the Kremlin-affiliated TV channel RT. The Russian news agency Tass informed thanks to hacker manipulations "Putin forces us to lie" and further "We urge you to stop this madness, do not send your sons and husbands to certain death."[117] The takeover was preceded by massive computer attacks against Ukrainian authorities and banks, behind which the Russians were suspected.[118]

Shortly after the invasion, hopes abounded that Putin might be expelled from office by his own compatriots. On 24 February 2022, i.e. on the very first day of the invasion, the Moscow journalist Yelena Chernenko wrote a statement that was signed shortly afterwards by almost 300 of her colleagues: "We, Russian correspondents and experts who write about Russian foreign policy, condemn the military operation launched by the Russian Federation in Ukraine," it said. War has never been a method of conflict resolution and never will be. There is no justification for this war. Within a few days, several similar calls were published in Russia. Artists, teachers, scientists and architects appealed to President Vladimir Putin to stop the bloodshed in the neighbouring country. Political scientist Tatyana Stanovaya of the Carnegie Moscow Center analysed that Putin does not have wide support among the elites for his war: "Of course, no one from the inner circle will oppose Putin now but the idea that the boss has gone mad is no longer the sole opinion of the liberal opposition".[119]

Indeed, in the days following the attack, thousands of people took to the streets of Russia to publicly protest against Putin's course of war. But the Moscow government cracked down: More than 3000 people were arrested during anti-war protests in 34 cities within a few days, according to the Russian human rights organisation OVD-Info.[120]

Three days after the invasion, Vladimir Putin activated the readiness of the so-called "deterrence forces". This indeed startled the world because, in addition to an arsenal of ballistic missiles, it included Russian nuclear weapons. However, the Stockholm-based peace research institute SIPRI announced after Putin's statements that it did not expect the war in Ukraine to lead to the use of nuclear weapons. "I do not think nuclear war is a likely outcome of this crisis," said SIPRI Director Dan Smith on 27 February 2022. He added: "If nuclear weapons exist, then unfortunately there is always this small possibility. And that would be catastrophic".[121]

Earlier, Russia had accused the West of scaremongering in response to warnings of nuclear war. "Everyone knows that a Third World War will be a nuclear war," said Russian Foreign Minister Sergei Lavrov. This question, however, is only a concern of Western politicians and not of the Russians.[122] Lavrov stressed: "We have a military doctrine that describes the parameters and conditions for the use of nuclear weapons." There will be no "escalation for the sake of de-escalation. But now there is talk about nuclear war". This is solely due to the West. He also accused Western states of "hysteria". In the same breath, the Russian foreign minister sharply criticised the USA: "The following comparisons come to mind: both Napoleon and Hitler once wanted to subjugate Europe. Now the Americans have subjugated it."[123] Nothing had ever so clearly marked the dividing line between the West and Russia before.

The West awakens

Russia's brutal attack on Ukraine in February 2022 was a wake-up call for the international community, especially for the West, i.e. North America and even more so Europe. It was not only a matter of taking Russia seriously but also of increasing its own defence capability.

In response, German Chancellor Olaf Scholz announced a massive increase in German defence spending. The 2022 federal budget should be endowed with a one-time special fund of 100 billion euros for "necessary investments and armament projects",

Scholz said in his government statement. He added: "We will invest more than two per cent of GDP in our defence from now on – year after year."

To reduce dependence on Russian natural gas, Scholz announced the construction of two terminals for liquefied natural gas (LNG) in Germany. Although there were many terminals for liquefied natural gas in the EU, Germany had none of its own.

Vladimir Putin's invasion of Ukraine on 24 February 2022, had been a wake-up call for Europe and Germany. Within a week, the EU proved to be more united than it had been for a long time. NATO announced that it would soon achieve its goal, which it had been fiddling with for years, that all member countries should spend two percent of their gross national product on defence. Sweden and Finland almost instantly discussed joining NATO. EU Commission President Ursula von der Leyen said of Ukraine's possible EU membership: "Over time, they are indeed one of us. They are one of us and we want them in." Shortly before, Ukrainian President Zelenskyy had declared: "We are turning to the EU for the immediate admission of Ukraine according to a new special procedure". This probably meant as quickly as possible.

In the Federal Republic, too, the clocks ran faster and the other way round in February 2022. Thus, Germany supplied weapons to a crisis area, something that had previously been non-negotiable. The federal government in office at the time, consisting of the SPD and the Greens, agreed to massively rearm the German Armed Forces within the shortest possible time. The SPD, Germany's peace party in its self-image, voted in favour of deploying unmanned combat air vehicles. Almost overnight, the Greens, the anti-nuclear and pro-environment party par excellence, began to reconsider the long since decided phase-out of nuclear and coal-fired power plants. Russian expansionism provoked a similar agile policy to that seen two years earlier in the coronavirus outbreak. To put it casually: If necessary, Germany, like other countries, can react surprisingly quickly and discard years of established dogma within a few days.

It was remarkable how not only the international community stood up to Russia and helped Ukraine in 2022 but also the business community. US multi-entrepreneur Elon Musk was a prime example of this. At the request of Ukrainian Digital Minister and Deputy Prime Minister Mychaylo Fedorov, Musk's company Starlink activated its satellite network over Ukraine to ensure internet coverage in the country. This meant that the country under attack had a functioning communications infrastructure, detached from Russian destruction.[124]

The courage of the Ukrainians and their president

Yet it was not only the international community and foreign entrepreneurs but above all the Ukrainians themselves who stunned the world with their courage and determination to repel the Russian military. The role model was Ukrainian President Volodymyr Zelenskyy, who declared a state of war after the launch of the Russian invasion and addressed the population with the following words:[125]

"Dear citizens of Ukraine,

This morning, President Putin declared the launch of a special military operation in the Donbass. Russia has attacked our military infrastructure and our border security forces. Explosions were heard in many cities.

We are introducing a state of war on the entire territory of our state. A minute ago, I had a conversation with President Biden. The US has already started to organise international support.

Today, composure is required – from each of you – if possible, please stay at home. We are working, the army is working, the whole defence and security sector are working. I, the National Security and Defence Council of Ukraine and the Cabinet of Ministers of Ukraine will be in constant contact with you.

I will be in touch again soon. No panic! We are strong and up for anything. We will defeat them all because we are Ukraine. Glory to Ukraine!"

A few hours later, he made another public appearance:

"My dear Ukrainians,

As promised, I will get back to you. I will give you up-to-date and reliable information every hour. We are now being attacked not only with bombs but also with fakes. It is important to get the truth from official sources.

Today Russia has started an invasion, Putin has started a war with Ukraine, with the whole democratic world. He wants to exterminate my state. He wants to annihilate our state - everything we had built, everything we live for.

I am addressing all Ukrainians, especially the military, who have already had to face the enemy's first attack and duly repel it: You are brave, you are unbroken, because you are Ukrainians.

I address every Ukrainian who is now on our soil: We should not panic; we should do everything necessary to support Ukraine's military.

I address all Ukrainians who are now abroad: We also need your support, you are a strong, united force, and you have also proven it time and time again, we need you now.

I have spoken to Biden, Johnson, Charles Michel, Duda, Nauseda – we are starting to form an anti-Putin coalition. We have called on world leaders to activate all possible sanctions against Putin, to initiate massive defence support, to close the air-space over Ukraine to the aggressor.

Together we must rescue Ukraine, rescue the democratic world – and we will. Glory to Ukraine!" [126]

The law graduate and former actor, dubbing artist, script-writer, television presenter, film producer and comedian matured into a political leader and war hero during the crisis.

However, both the USA and the EU categorically rejected military intervention by the West to support Ukraine. Harsh words, tough sanctions and even arms deliveries – that had to suffice. The danger of unleashing a "big war" if they actually intervened in Ukraine seemed too great.

Nevertheless, Moscow's effort to present the "Ukraine question" as a kind of sideshow was a complete failure in the face of opposition at home and abroad. Vladimir Putin had completely underestimated the impact of his invasion of Ukraine. He had obviously assumed that, just as with his "adventures" in Syria, Georgia and Libya, as well as in Crimea, the West would "grumble" a little but ultimately accept the new situation he had created.

China's tightrope walk to diplomacy

However, it was not only Germany and Europe – to say the least of the USA – who regarded the Russian invasion of Ukraine as tantamount to crossing a red line. On 2 March 2022, at an extraordinary United Nations General Assembly, 141 countries approved a UN resolution condemning the Russian invasion of Ukraine. They called on Moscow to "immediately, completely and unconditionally withdraw all of its military forces from the territory of Ukraine within its internationally recognized borders". Only Belarus, Eritrea, North Korea and Syria vetoed the motion. Even traditional friends of Russia like Cuba and Serbia did not support the Russian attack – nor did China.

The People's Republic of China abstained from voting on the UN resolution, as it had previously done in the UN Security Council. The fact that Beijing did not defend Moscow's position caused other non-Western states, which always stand by China, to also refuse to support Russia.

At the same time, China's foreign office spokesperson Wang Wenbin made it clear that China and Russia are "strategic partners" but not "allies". China decides its attitude and policy on a case-by-case basis. All sides should remain calm, show restraint and avoid further escalation," was the message from Beijing. This disengagement was probably caused mainly by the fact that Vladimir Putin had threatened to use nuclear weapons if the West interfered militarily in Ukraine. For China wants to be perceived as a peacemaker in the world, as a level-headed world power that is concerned about balance and moderation, and that has the well-being of all states around the globe at heart. Therefore, open support for the Russian aggressor Putin was out of the question for Beijing in 2022.

But there can be no doubt that China remains committed to Russia as a partner – even as a "junior partner" – in competition with the United States of America. So, it was only consistent in 2022 not to praise Russia for the invasion of Ukraine but not to condemn the invasion either. While the assembled West quickly agreed on sanctions, Beijing vehemently rejected such steps. Rather, the People's Republic of China supported Moscow's narrative that NATO's successive eastward expansion had disregarded Russia's "legitimate" security needs and that the West had thus provoked the war.

Officially, China justified its abstention on the UN resolution against Russia by saying that it had not "taken into account the history and complexity of the current crisis". The wording was backed by Beijing's position that NATO and the US had caused the war and that a peaceful solution would require Russia's demands for security guarantees to be met, in particular the assurance that Ukraine would not join either the EU or NATO. The Chinese ambassador to the UN, Zhang Jun, described the resolution as "blind pressure" that would only serve to escalate the situation further. As morally justified as Russia's condemnation by the international community may have been, China's representative was right in the matter.

For China was hardly interested in a major war, at least at that juncture. Just two days after the invasion of Ukraine by Russian troops, Chinese UN Ambassador Zhang Jun had stated: "We have now reached a point we do not want to see." China's Foreign Minister Wang Yi declared that the People's Republic respects the sovereignty and territorial integrity of all countries – including Ukraine.Only shortly before, Moscow and Beijing had demonstratively rallied together at the opening of the 2022 Winter Olympics and declared a "borderless" partnership.

In this state of equilibrium, China functioned as a conciliatory mediator. After a telephone conversation between Xi Jinping and Vladimir Putin, Russia declared itself ready for talks with Ukraine. China celebrated this as a success in the role of mediator. Chinese Foreign Ministry spokesperson Wang Wenbin stressed: "China's approach is in significant contrast to the practice of other countries that cause crises, fuel them or even profit from them. On the question of which approach to Europe's security and stability is the right one, I think we will all come to a fair conclusion."

The aim of the tightrope act was obviously not to violate the partnership with Russia, to put a stop to the advance of the USA and at the same time not to snub Europe as a partner. At the beginning of March 2022, China's Foreign Minister Wang Yi described Russia as its most important strategic partner, notwithstanding the Ukraine war. The bond with Moscow, he said, is one of the most important bilateral relations in the world and the friendship between the two peoples is unquestionable: "No matter how threatening the international situation may be, we will maintain our strategic alignment and promote the development of a comprehensive partnership between China and Russia in the new era." In the "new era", Beijing has the entire world in mind:

Cooperation is not only beneficial to the peoples of both countries, "but also contributes to peace, stability and development in the world". Thus the Chinese foreign minister explained his country's policy in 2022.[127]

"Alliance Treaty" between China and Russia 2022

On 4 February 2022, shortly before the Russian invasion of Ukraine, Russian President Vladimir Putin and Chinese President Xi Jinping concluded an "alliance agreement" in Beijing.

Historians compared the alliance of the two communist states in 2022 with the rapprochement of the USA and China under US President Richard Nixon during his historic visit to China in 1972.Nixon's visit to Mao Zedong was a defining moment in Cold War history. After all, relations between China and the Soviet Union were extremely poor at the time. The divide between the two communist states had begun in 1956, when Nikita Khrushchev distanced himself from Stalin at the 20th Congress of the Communist Party. This speech and Khrushchev's destalinisation campaign angered Mao, who condemned it as revisionist, probably fearing that one day he would be ostracised in his country in the same way that Stalin was by Khrushchev in Russia. The ideological and political differences of opinion led to the Sino-Soviet discord in 1960. Nine years later, Soviet and Chinese forces fought fierce battles along the Ussuri River near Northeast China. A more extensive war could only be averted with great difficulty.

The US President at the time, Richard Nixon, had seen the rift between the two communist powers as an opportunity to gain a new ally in China in the midst of the Cold War between the USA and the Soviet Union. It was in this vein that Air Force One with Richard Nixon landed in Beijing at 11.30 a.m. on 21 February 1972.It was arguably one of the most audacious diplomatic missions of the twentieth century. For at that time, the victory of the communists in the Chinese civil war, the fatalities of the Korean and Vietnam wars and almost a quarter of a century of mutual curses stood between Washington and Beijing. The "Great Proletarian Cultural Revolution", Mao's gigantic and murderous political campaign, had reached its climax but in the USA, China appeared alongside the Soviet Union as the epitome of inhuman communism. The rapprochement of the two countries was a diplomatic and a geopolitical sensation. "None of us could have imagined then where China is today," says diplomat Winston Lord later, who travelled to Beijing with Nixon at the time and later became US ambassador to China. "But given its sheer size, history and culture, one circumstance could be certain: that there would be no stable world until China had a share in it". [128] This was undoubtedly a wise insight but it also applies to Russia.

At that time, it was certainly thanks to the scenario of a two-front war by the Soviet Union – against NATO in the West and against China in the East – evoked by Nixon that the USSR agreed to a policy of détente with the USA. The then Russian President Leonid Brezhnev even went as far as to sign the Helsinki Accords, which enabled the West to challenge Soviet totalitarianism on the basis of human rights.

Just as the Soviet Union was the big loser of the Sino-American rapprochement of 1972, Russia is likely to prove the big loser of the agreement between Putin and Xi in 2022. China has long regarded itself as the only superpower in the world that can seriously stand up to the USA. For China, Russia is merely a junior partner in the global power poker, at best suitable for tying up the military forces of the West. After all, Russia still has significantly more military strength, especially in terms of nuclear weapons, than China.

In addition, Russia is an attractive supplier of raw materials for China. The natural gas that does not flow westwards towards Europe is welcome in China, which is desperate for energy. All Siberian raw material deposits, which Russia needed Western capital and know-how to develop, would be exclusively available to China if the Russian economy were isolated from the West. Putin, in closing ranks with Xi in 2022, no doubt weighed in on the assumption that this partnership would help him in his confrontation with the West. But from China's point of view, Putin was and is more of a "useful idiot" to bring Russia into a vassal-like dependence on China.[129]

Millions flee Ukraine

As a result of the Russian attack on Ukraine, the EU prepared for around seven million refugees from the stricken country. In order to help them quickly and without bureaucracy, the "Temporary Protection" directive from 2001 was activated. This guarantees war refugees up to three years of protection in the EU without a complex asylum procedure.

In 2022, in the face of the Russian threat, all EU states drew closer together than they had done for a long time. German Interior Minister Nancy Faeser said after a meeting with her EU colleagues."All EU states are ready to accept war refugees from Ukraine. This is a strong European response to the terrible suffering Putin is causing with his criminal war of aggression."

The corresponding directive is a consequence of the wars in the former Yugoslavia in the 1990s. It had never been used before 2022 – not even during the great exodus of 2015 and 2016. In total, at least 15 countries with at least 65 per cent of the EU population must agree to make the directive valid and applicable. The minimum standards that all EU countries must guarantee include, for example, a work permit for displaced persons as well as access to social assistance, medical care, education for minors and, under certain conditions, the possibility of family reunification.[130]

Poland, for example, a country that had vehemently refused to welcome refugees from Syria, welcomed the Ukrainian refugees with open arms in 2022. Three days after the war began, Poland had already registered around 200,000 refugees from their besieged neighbour. At that time, that was more than half of all the people who had fled Ukraine. One week after the start of the war, around 10,000 people had died and more than one million had fled the country.[131] Every day in February and March 2022, tens of thousands of new refugees arrived in Poland and were welcomed with open arms. Many Poles donated and organised relief goods: clothes, blankets and food – everything by way of humanitarian aid that people who have fled head over heels need.[132] The refugee flow also arrived in Germany, where the willingness to help was also extremely high in these weeks and months.

Vladimir Putin: "The weak get beaten"

The attack on Ukraine in February 2022 came as a surprise only to those who had not been observing Russian President Vladimir Putin closely enough. For he has always been a man of brute force.

Vladimir Putin grew up in the cramped milieu of a communal flat in Saint Petersburg, which was then still called Leningrad. He lived with his family in a room of about 20 square metres, without running water; an improvised kitchen was in the hallway. During these years, the boy spent his time in the backyards of the district. According to former friends, in adolescent years he frequently got into fights and always exhibited extreme aggression. He himself confirmed in his memoirs: "You had to demonstrate strength in every case – regardless of whether you were right or not. Because the weak get beaten".

At the age of eleven, Putin started his favourite sport, sambo, a martial art with roots in Japanese judo. One of his teachers was Leonid Usvyazov, a criminal who had served almost 20 years behind bars, including for gang rape. In his memoirs, Putin shows great compassion for the man who was killed in a criminal confrontation in 1994.

At 17, Vladimir Putin enlisted in the KGB, which he probably considered the only strong organisation in the Soviet Union at the time. By all accounts, he had never attracted any particular attention there – except for his persistence. This coincides with a judgement that ex-president Boris Yeltsin later made about his successor: He had experienced Putin as "militarily tough and steadfast".[133]

The former intelligence officer came to power in 1999/2000 with an exceedingly brutal war at home, against breakaway Chechnya infiltrated by Islamist forces.

At the latest since then, he had been mourning the once powerful Soviet Union. In a film shortly before the 2018 presidential election, he said the West wanted to give Russia the seat but that did not suit Moscow. From his memories of fighting in the Leningrad backyards where he grew up, he told the story of a rat that he had cornered and that chased him afterwards. It even tried to jump on his head. In his own words that taught him a lesson .[134] This should probably translate into Putin's idea of world politics: If you have the power to destroy an enemy, destroy him before he dances on your head. In various positions of power, Putin has had dealings with five US presidents to date; after the departure of German Chancellor Angela Merkel in 2021, Vladimir Putin has since become the most experienced head of state in Europe.

Putin captures the hearts of the Germans

Before 2022, however, Putin often acted strategically and with tactical skill, with a sense of the right timing to achieve successes. For example, the Kremlin leader captured the hearts of many Germans during a state visit to Germany together with his wife Ludmilla in autumn 2001. On 25 September 2001, following a welcome by the then President of the Bundestag, Wolfgang Thierse, and signing the guest book of the German Bundestag, he gave a speech to the members of the Bundestag and the Bundesrat that oozed peace and the offer to cooperate sounded sincere and convincing.

It is probably still thanks to memories of that time that there are so many "Putin-sympathizers" in Germany, people who see the American drive for power as the cause of almost all evil in the world and who more or less classify Russia's war of aggression against Ukraine in 2022 as Moscow's "self-defence" to defend itself against the "encirclement" of the US-dominated NATO. Putin always managed to be friendly and obliging as well as equally brutal and unpredictable.

Back then, in 2001, he had still declared that he "recognised NATO's role in the world. If we change the quality of relations between NATO and Russia, NATO enlargement will no longer be a significant issue." Later, he was generous about the Baltic countries joining NATO: "We can't forbid them to make their choice if they want to improve their security in a special way."

But with Russia's alienation from the West and the decline of the Russian economy, Putin changed his strategy: NATO was henceforth the hated enemy, which he threatened first with deceit and since 2022 with open combat.

The coup d'état-like annexation of Crimea and the intervention in Syria were examples of skilful tactics. But in 2022, he abandoned this path of underhanded tactics and embarked on the path of brute force. Possibly it was because, at nearly 70 years of age, he had concluded that gradual advancement would not enable him to restore the former power of the Soviet Union in time to live to see it.[135]

Bounty on Vladimir Putin's head

With the undisguised attack on Ukraine, Vladimir Putin endangered his own position as Russia's head of state. For the subsequent sanctions by the EU and the USA hit Russia hard. Besides the general population, the oligarchs who had become rich over the years were also affected. The billionaire business tycoons had to watch helplessly as their yachts were confiscated, their assets frozen and their freedom to travel destroyed overnight, so that they suddenly had nothing at all left of their dream villas in Europe. After the EU rushed ahead with sanctions, US President Joe Biden declared: "We will join our European partners and confiscate your yachts, your luxury apartments and your private jets. We are coming for your ill-begotten gains". Putin himself had his yacht "Graceful" quickly shipped from the Hamburg shipyard "Blohm + Voss" to Kaliningrad at the beginning of February before his war of aggression.[136]

But the oligarchs literally paid a high price for the lust for power of the supreme warlord in the Kremlin, from which they could not make any profit. Against this backdrop, the West's hope in 2022 was that the Russian tycoons would oust Putin in a coup d'état and end the war in Ukraine. This hope was nourished when the Russian entrepreneur Alexander Konanykhin put a bounty on Vladimir Putin's head about a week after the war began. On his Facebook page, he displayed Putin on a Wild West poster with the words "Wanted Dead or Alive" and wrote: "I promise to pay $1,000,000 to the officer(s) who, complying with their constitutional duty, arrest(s) Putin as a war criminal under Russian and international laws. Putin is not the Russian president as he came to power as the result of a special operation of blowing up apartment buildings in Russia, then violated the Constitution by eliminating free elections and murdering his opponents. As an ethnic Russian and a Russian citizen, I see it as my moral duty to facilitate the denazification of Russia. I will continue my assistance to Ukraine in its heroic efforts to withstand the onslaught of Putin's Orda".[137] The post was online not long before it was deleted – though not by the Russian government but by Facebook. While the entire Western world was trying to stop the despot and people were dying daily in the turmoil of war in Ukraine, Facebook insisted that such a call for "tyrannicide" contradicted the general terms and conditions of the world's largest social network.

Sanctions against Russia: China learns its lessons

At the National People's Congress held at the beginning of March 2022, the People's Republic of China drew its first lessons from the West's sanctions against Russia following the invasion of Ukraine a few days earlier. The most important one was to further reduce China's dependence on the West. The Cross-Border Interbank Payment System (Cips), the Chinese alternative to the international payment system Swift, plays a key role here. When Cips was launched in 2015, 19 banks participated, including Deutsche Bank, Citibank, HSBC and Standard Chartered. Cips entered 2022 with 1,280 financial service providers from 103 countries. By way of comparison, the Swift organisation, founded in 1973, has 11,000 financial institutions from around 200 countries. The differences are therefore (still) huge: Swift manages about 50 million transactions per day, while Cips only manages 15,000.

In 2014, after the annexation of Crimea, Russia launched its own system, SPFS (System for Transfer of Financial Messages), which, however, lags far behind technologically and only works during office hours instead of around the clock like Cips and Swift. The Chinese Cips system is capable of processing SPFS transactions.[138] So the Swift ban on Russian banks in spring 2022 could drive droves of new customers into the arms of the Chinese financial system.

However, Beijing has done everything in the fight over Ukraine and refrained from doing anything that could drag China itself into the war. For at that time, China by no means wanted to start a "great war" with the West but rather to make the world its own with strategic alliances, for example via the Silk Road project, and in an economic and technological race. Xi Jinping, General Secretary of the Communist Party of China since 2012 and President of the People's Republic since 2013, had long since understood that US supremacy was based not only on military superiority but almost as much on economic power, innovative capacity and the accompanying technological pioneering role.

Economic and techno-war

To understand China's quest for power and its seemingly irrepressible urge to challenge the US for global supremacy, a comparative look at the figures is useful. It becomes clear that China is economically more successful. Exports of goods already massively [139] exceeded the $2.5 trillion mark in 2020, while the US was well below $1.5 trillion. [140] In terms of foreign exchange reserves, the economic disparity becomes even more obvious: as of 2020, China had more than 3.2 trillion US dollars in foreign exchange,[141] compared to a paltry 140 billion dollars in the US.[142] China is also in the lead in terms of economic growth: in the USA it was 5.3 percent in 2021, while China came in at 8.1 percent. For 2022, China expects 5.5 per cent, the USA 4 per cent.[143]

The humbling experience

In his book "Dealing with China", former US Secretary of the Treasury Henry Paulson recounts what he calls "one of the most humbling moments" in his life: It was a meeting with China's Vice Premier Wang Qishan in June 2008 near the US capital Washington. The United States economy was then about three times the size of that in China but it was declining in a dramatic downward spiral. The entire financial system was close to the abyss, and a few months later the investment bank Lehman Brothers collapsed. Yet not only the fiscal crisis, but the real estate market was also shaken; unemployment and public debt climbed to staggering heights. At that time, Wang Qishan is reputed to have said to Henry Paulson: "You were my teacher, but now here I am in my teacher's domain, and look at your system, Hank. We aren't sure we should be learning from you anymore". Paulson writes about this in his book: "At that time, the relationship between our two countries began to shift noticeably as the U.S.'s troubles brought doubt and discredit to our system in some quarters and boosted China's self-confidence". Since then, China's economic output has roughly tripled and its foreign exchange reserves have doubled. The trade surplus with the US, then about $270 billion, passed the $400 billion mark in 2020.[144]

From the American perspective, China has fought its way up by unfair means. Although China has been a member of the World Trade Organisation (WTO) since 2001, it still does not abide by its rules, the USA complains. The accusations are that market access in China is regulated, intellectual theft of Western expertise is rampant and Chinese companies are supported with massive state aid for their global expansion. To counter this development, the US opened a trade war against China in 2018. In July 2018, it imposed a first tranche of punitive tariffs on imports from China, in August the second, and in September the third. China initially responded with similar retaliatory measures. The trade war was on. But Beijing soon ran out of imports on which it could impose punitive tariffs in the first place. China imports less from the US less than a quarter of what it exports there. When Trump and Xi agreed on a 90-day tariff freeze at the G20 summit in early December 2018, trade peace seemed fleetingly within grasp. But shortly afterwards, Meng Wanzhou, the chief financial officer of the Chinese telecom company, was arrested in Vancouver and Washington demanded his extradition. Shortly before Christmas 2018, the US Department of Justice charged two Chinese with infiltrating American internet companies and US Department of Energy facilities. China was already preparing for a further escalation. In 2018 alone, Beijing lowered the reserve requirement for Chinese banks four times to pump money into the market and replenish its war chest for the trade conflict. China also worked hard on the RCEP agreement, a trade pact with the other Pacific economies. The RCEP area comprises about 45 per cent of the world's population and more than one third of world trade. The year 2018 marked a change in strategy that has continued so far and is likely to last until 2049.

China began to rely on a strategy that had actually seemed obsolete since the go-it-alone days of the Mao era: the path to autarky. In the technology sector in particular, dependence on the US was far too high in the face of a looming trade war. For many years, the division was quite clear: goods were produced incessantly in China and consumed just as incessantly in America. The development of the products took place in the USA because that was the home of creativity, entrepreneurship, venture capital and also technological leadership. China formed a kind of extended workbench. As early as 2006, the historian Niall Ferguson coined the term "Chimerica" for this. This symbiosis not only worked economically for both sides but was also a peace-stabilising element. Beijing's pursuit of its own excellence in the technology sector increasingly undermined this interaction.

China has not yet drawn, or even hinted at, what is probably the most potent weapon in an economic confrontation with the US up to 2022: the sale of its US government bonds. Among financial experts, this measure is called the "nuclear option" because it has the potential to endanger the entire global economy, so beyond the US, it also includes China itself. In such a financial war, the question would probably no longer be who wins it but rather who loses faster. True to Mao Zedong's motto: "You wage your war. I'll wage mine".

It is a kind of "economic iron curtain", as former US Secretary of the Treasury Henry Paulson called it. Similar to the Cold War after World War II, such a division of the world into two power blocs forces all other states to choose sides. The New Silk Road concept is nothing more than China's attempt to win over large parts of the world – especially Europe and Africa – to its side. In doing so, however, the Chinese are relying on economic connections in keeping with the times.

As early as the beginning of November 2018, the then US Secretary of the Treasury Henry Paulson spoke plainly: If the US and China cannot find a way to develop a workable consensus, it will pose a systemic risk of monumental proportions — not just to the global economy, as I dealt with, but to international order as we know it and to world peace". Since then, the situation has not changed for the better – on the contrary, the Corona situation in 2020/21 has rather made things worse.

The new Silk Road – a dream comes true

Probably no project illustrates the rise and the claim to power of modern China as strongly as the project "The New Silk Road".

In 2013, Chinese leader Xi Jinping presented his "Chinese dream" of the "great rebirth of the Chinese nation" and launched the Silk Road project in this context. In reference to the ancient Silk Road, he named his pet project the Belt and Road Initiative

(BRI). The Chinese term "Yi Dai Yi Lu" (The Belt and Road Initiative) means "One Belt" or "One Belt" and "One Road". This refers to the Silk Roads, which have been used to transport goods and ideas from east to west and west to east across the Eurasian landmass and across the sea for more than two thousand years. China's strategic interest in "Yi Dai Yi Lu", the energy sector – oil, natural gas, coal – and in other natural resources were obvious from the beginning.

The gigantic project of the century is expected to encompass over three billion people, well over half the world's population. China plans to invest $900 billion in the project over the 2020s. In the long term, the investment volume is estimated at 5,000 to 8,000 billion dollars. The focus is on investment in infrastructure, true to the old Chinese proverb "If you want to get rich in trade, start by building a road". More than 100 countries have directly or indirectly joined this initiative.

The Silk Road as an East-West trade route dates back to the second century BC. Silk was the most traded commodity at that time. In Rome, as the Roman philosopher Seneca already remarked, the soft, "almost transparent" cloth was bought and worn in "ever greater quantities". Soon silk was not only a sought-after commodity but also a means of payment alongside coins and grain.

The new Silk Road is much more extensive than the historical one. The Silk Road of the nineteenth century referred to an ancient network of caravan routes whose main route connected the Mediterranean region with East Asia by land via Central Asia. The term goes back to the nineteenth century German geographer Ferdinand von Richthofen, who first used it in 1877. The new Silk Road extends beyond Asia and Europe to the African continent.

When today's China speaks of the "New Silk Road", it is also a term of revenge for the plundering and humiliation of that time, because the modern Silk Road project has one primary goal: to extend China's power to Europe in the broadest sense.

Railways, roads, bridges, tunnels, ports, pipelines, airports, power plants and universities are to be built and renewed along the new route. From Beijing to Rome, from Laos to Morocco, from Chongqing to Duisburg, from Moscow to Korea, from the Taklamakan Desert in China to the steppes of Central Asia and the desert of North Africa, or from Fuzhou to Rotterdam. There is talk of a win-win situation from which China itself but also all the countries involved in the project, are to benefit.

China's charm offensive in the West

In 2018, Portugal and Greece became the first countries in Europe to sign a New Silk Road cooperation agreement with China. The first case involves investments in the expansion of the Portuguese Atlantic port of Sines. Portugal's Prime Minister António Costa said: "We want the port of Sines to become part of the new maritime Silk Road. Sines is Portugal's Atlantic port with the largest growth capacity. It is a deep seaport located in close proximity to major sea routes from the Mediterranean, Atlantic and Southern Africa. Sines can become the European interface of these maritime routes. It is enormously important for trade relations between Europe and Asia that Portugal becomes part of the new Silk Road."

In the process, Portugal wants to position its own port as a lock gate for Europe by building a new modern railway line to the Spanish border. The goods arriving at the port of Sines are to reach the Spanish capital Madrid quickly from 2023 – and thus also the European rail corridor Madrid-Paris-Berlin.

Portugal does not seem to have any reserves about maintaining contact with China. Ever since the fiscal crisis, when the Portuguese government privatised state-owned enterprises, Chinese investors have owned almost nine per cent of Portugal's listed companies, with a focus on banking and insurance as well as energy supply. The reverse route works less well: only 1.2 per cent of Portuguese exports go to China – and the very largest share comes from the Volkswagen plant Autoeuropa, part of the German VW Group, just outside Lisbon.[145]

In Greece, the Chinese state-owned shipping company Cosco has been the majority shareholder of the Piraeus Port Authority (PPA) since 2016. For 280.5 million euros, Cosco bought 51 percent of the previously state-owned port company PPA. In return, the Chinese company is allowed to operate several container, car and passenger terminals in Piraeus until 2052. The deal was part of the privatisation programme that the EU and the International Monetary Fund demanded of Greece in the wake of the debt crisis. China seized this opportunity to gain and expand a central bridgehead to Europe on the outskirts of the Greek capital Athens. In total, the Chinese want to invest 350 million euros directly in the port facilities by 2026 and another 200 million euros in affiliated projects, for example the conversion of old warehouse buildings into luxury hotels. It is apparently typical for China to choose countries for such investments that are in economically difficult circumstances but offer bargains with a lot of potential. Piraeus is the first natural deepwater port that container ships from Asia reach in Europe after passing through the Suez Canal in Egypt. So, it is ideal for China to establish this very port as a hub of its new Silk Road. Since the entry of the Chinese, Piraeus has been the fastest growing port in the world. In the next step, a railway line will connect Piraeus via Skopje and Belgrade to Budapest, i.e. to the heart of Central Europe. This transport route would be an alternative to the inconvenient sea route via the Strait of Gibraltar past Spain and France to finally land in Hamburg or Rotterdam. The goods train from Piraeus to Budapest takes two days, the container ship to Hamburg one week.[146] Piraeus as a port of entry into Europe is thus an extremely clever choice on China's part.

The expansion of the railway line between Piraeus and Budapest should also be seen strategically: China wants to find access to the heart of Europe above all via the economically relatively weak countries of Eastern Europe. The largest steel plant in Serbia, the powerful Romanian coal-fired power plant in Rovinari, the largest Romanian oil refinery, the Albanian oil field Patos-Marinza, the international airport of the Albanian capital Tirana – all these have been bought by Chinese companies. In all cases, the companies are either Chinese state-owned enterprises or private companies with state participation.

There is ample evidence that China is harnessing its burgeoning power in countries like Greece to exert political pressure. Greece is one of the best or worst examples of this. Since the Chinese entered Piraeus, the government in Athens has voted several times in favour of China in important decisions within the

EU, explicitly opposing the other EU member states. For example, in summer 2016, the Greek government blocked a joint EU statement condemning China's aggressive behaviour in the South China Sea. In June 2017, it prevented the EU from officially rebuking China's human rights policies in a report. A few days later, Athens opposed tougher conditions for Chinese investment in the EU. A clear connection to Chinese investments cannot be proven but the voting behaviour of the Greek government is certainly an indication of dependence.[147]

Italy at the helm, the European dwarfs to follow

In 2019, Italy became the first G7 country to sign a Memorandum of Understanding (MoU) with China to participate in the new Silk Road. To be precise, there were 29 declarations of intent with investment commitments from China to Italy amounting to 2.5 billion euros. The most important commitments concerned two Italian ports: In Trieste, the Chinese construction company CCCC wants to improve the connections to Eastern and Central Europe, and in Genoa, cooperation is planned for the enlargement of the port. The total potential of the agreement was estimated at around 20 billion euros.[148]

In the other EU countries, Italy's move was viewed rather critically, as was the press, which ran headlines along the lines of "Italy – a Chinese gateway to Europe?

Switzerland became the fourth country in the European Schengen area to join the new Silk Road in 2019. According to reports, the Swiss have demanded a commitment to human rights from China in return. When this second agreement proved futile, the government relented, it says.[149]

China-Monaco connection is model for cooperation with all of Europe" was the headline of the "Belt & Road News", a Chinese publication that reports on everything going on along the New Silk Road. On the occasion of the new Silk Road, Xi Jinping was the first Chinese president to visit the rich dwarf state in Europe. He was received by Prince Albert in the palace like a monarch. It says a lot about the importance of the new Silk Road for China that the president of the East Asian giant empire with 1.4 billion people visited the second-smallest state on earth with a population of 38,000. "Monaco is a pacesetter and role model for our relations with Europe," said Xi Jinping. China's most powerful man wants to involve as many as possible, preferably all European states, in its Belt and Road Initiative.[150]

17 plus 1

Eastern Europe plays a crucial role in China's plan to become a global superpower. Since 2012, the concept "16 + 1" has been synonymous with 16 countries in Eastern Europe, eleven of them in the European Union, and "1" with China. Greece joined in April 2019 and since then there have been 17 plus 1 states.

What is the hallmark of the 17+1 countries in the Chinese plan? The answer is clear: in these countries, China wants to exert long-term economic and political influence by investing in infrastructure – and ultimately repress the influence of Washington, Berlin or Paris. This clearly distinguishes the 17+1 Group from Germany or France, for example, where China's aim is to gain access to know-how through company investments and acquisitions and, as far as possible, to take over technologically relevant companies. Germany is home to a substantial number of so-called "hidden champions", companies that are rather unknown outside their respective industries, some of which have a global market share of more than 50 percent within their sector. For China, these companies represent a strategically extremely interesting prey. The situation is different in the 17+1 region, where China uses its money to lure the less developed and rather poorer countries with attractive investment promises. Roads, bridges, ports, railway lines, telecommunications networks, power plants – the list of Chinese-supported infrastructure projects in Eastern Europe is long. Often, these are projects that have not been classified by the EU as eligible for funding. The best example of this is Poland, which received more than one billion in direct investment from China between 2000 and 2018. This is also related to the forecast that Poland will probably soon stop receiving subsidies from Brussels and will move from being a net recipient to a net payer in the EU by 2027 at the latest. At the same time, Poland is dependent on the USA as a security guarantor in order to feel somewhat protected from its large neighbour Russia. Following Russia's annexation of the Ukrainian Republic of Crimea in 2014, it has become clear that Russia does not want to settle for its status quo on the world stage, not even territorially. Thus, Poland is walking a dangerous tightrope between the power blocs, ultimately with the goal of political independence and economic prosperity.

But as the term 17+1 suggests, Poland is not alone in Eastern Europe with 1.4 billion direct investments from China between 2000 and 2018. Hungary leads with 2.4 billion euros in the same period, followed by Poland, the Czech Republic (1.0 billion euros), Romania (900 million euros), Bulgaria (400 million), Slovenia and Croatia with 300 million euros each, and Slovakia, Lithuania, Latvia, and Estonia with 100 million euros each. For all these countries, these millions represent huge sums of money to move their economies forward. For China, on the other hand, it is comparatively manageable amounts to secure economic and political influence.

How energetically the People's Republic of China intends to forge ahead with at least the economic conquest of the world in the 2020s can probably be seen from the chutzpah with which it presented by far the largest free trade agreement in the world at the end of 2020 under the name "Regional Comprehensive Economic Partnership" (RCEP). It was a major geopolitical event: China and 14 Asian countries signed a treaty that covers a third of world trade and economies that are home to 2.2 billion people. In addition to China, the newly created free trade zone includes the countries Japan, South Korea, Australia and New Zealand as well as the ten ASEAN countries Indonesia, Malaysia, the Philippines, Singapore, Thailand, Vietnam, Cambodia, Laos, Myanmar and Brunei.[151]

Economic warfare has long been in full swing

The rejection of multilateralism and the resurgence of bilateralism are also evident in the economic sector. A typical example of this is the trade war raging between China and the USA. The exchange of goods between the United States and China amounted to around 635 billion US dollars in 2017, with the People's Republic posting a trade surplus of almost 376 billion US dollars.[152] Given these figures, there is indeed no denying the disproportion of trade relations that encouraged the US administration to launch a trade war in 2018. In summer 2018, for example, the US government presented a lengthy list of tariffs, mainly on food and consumer goods from China. In total, annual imports of these goods would have been worth 200 billion US dollars at last count.[153]

In the run-up to the annual meeting of the G20 countries at the end of November 2018, it became public that the then US President Donald Trump wanted to conclude a bilateral trade agreement with the president of the world's second largest economy, Xi Jinping. The trigger for this – as was not unusual in Trump's style of governing at the time – was an extensive phone call between the two leaders on 1 November 2018, which Trump described as "long and very good": "We talked about many issues, with a clear focus on trade". However, anyone who believed that this was the end of the trade war between China and the US underestimated both the fickleness of the former US president and the fundamental conflict between the two nations.

Since the 2020/21 pandemic, it has become obvious that a "New Cold War" is underway between China and the US, which will presumably last throughout the 2020s and heat up beyond this decade.[154] As in the first Cold War, the USA is on one side, only on the other side the adversary has changed: the Soviet Union the first time, China in particular the second time, albeit with a resurgent Russia. It is certainly no coincidence that in both cases the regime is communist. Democracy and communism as two fundamental counter-designs of a state structure are diametrically opposed to each other; this also holds true under US President Joe Biden.

UN Secretary-General António Guterres, meanwhile, warned at the 75th United Nations General Assembly in 2020: "We are moving in an extremely dangerous direction. Our world cannot afford a future where the two largest economies split the globe". This would create a technological and economic divide that could escalate into a military divide. Everything would have to be done to avoid further escalation.[155] It is to be feared that this warning will receive little attention in the 2020s.

US stock markets without China

Regardless of whether this happens or not, the very idea of barring Chinese companies from US stock exchanges would cause massive distress in the economic world. Chinese corporations would be isolated from US investors, and US investors from lucrative financial investments in China. Nevertheless, the US government threatened this very measure in 2019 as another escalation stage in the trade war. China promptly warned that US economic protectionism could plunge the world into a recession. Tariffs and provoked trade conflicts serve to "undermine the global economic and trade order", Chinese Foreign Minister Wang Yi clearly warned before the 2019 UN General Assembly in New York. He said they wanted to resolve issues in a calm and reasonable manner, to add: "However, should the other side act in bad faith or show no respect for equal status or role in the negotiations, we must take the necessary measures to uphold our legitimate right and interest".[156]

Big business in China from Apple to BioNTech

For both US and European companies, any trade conflict with China poses a severe problem because Americans and Europeans do immense business in China. For example, in the third quarter of 2021, in the midst of the pandemic and US President Joe Biden's tougher tones against China, Apple posted a 36 per cent expansion in revenue to around $81 billion and a doubling in profit to nearly $22 billion.[157] That was impressive but it was also impossible not to notice that the strongest growth resulted from China: there, Apple's sales rose by a staggering 58 per cent to almost €15 billion in the third quarter of 2021.[158] In order not to jeopardise its business, Apple has been kowtowing to the power centre in Beijing for years. In order not to anger government authorities, the company has apparently made far-reaching concessions with regard to data protection, security and censorship. Among other things, the access code for user data for Chinese customers are not managed in the USA but in Chinese data centres by a local state-owned company.[159] In other words, the iCorporation, which otherwise strongly insists on privacy, is allowing Beijing to access the personal data of Chinese Apple customers This is just one of many examples – albeit a particularly striking one, after all Apple is considered the most valuable company in the world – of how Western companies subordinate themselves to Chinese government policy in order to profit from the huge volume of business in the most populous state in East Asia.

A similarly striking example of this, albeit from Europe, is the pharmaceutical manufacturer BioNTech. In the midst of the 2021 pandemic, when vaccine became a life-saving elixir, BioNTech backed down on vaccine shipments to Taiwan out of deference to the political power centre in China.[160] A delivery volume of five million vaccine doses had already been agreed before Beijing intervened.[161] Apple and BioNTech, the most valuable corporation in the world and arguably the best vaccine provider in the world against the coronavirus, do not dare to act openly against China but cave in so as not to jeopardise their business interests. The shareholders of both companies may be happy about this but at the same time it says a lot about China's position of power in the world since the beginning of the 2020s.

China's path to cutting-edge technology

When the US government banned Chinese technology company Huawei in 2019, it was primarily an attempt to prevent China's long technological march to the top of the world. After all, Huawei had risen to become the second largest producer of smartphones. The announcement by Chinese President Xi Jinpi to put China at the forefront of technology was not just political talk but a seriously pursued strategy. This is by no means only true for smartphones but in many areas. There are numerous examples of this; the fact that the Chinese space probe "Chang'e 4" succeeded in making the first landing on the far side of the moon exemplifies the fact that China is vying for supremacy far beyond Mother Earth.

In the middle of the coronavirus pandemic year 2021, China surprised the technology world with its own CPU, a Central Processing Unit, which has a self-developed set of instructions. To understand the dimension of this development, one must know that CPUs, often called microprocessors, are the basis of every kind of computer. This is not only about hardware but above all about software. Under the name *Loongson Architecture*, China 2021 presented its own set of instructions, a kind of programming language for microprocessors, for the first time. Previously, the Chinese computer industry had always used the processor language MIPS64, which was developed in the USA.[162] Piquant detail: While China was still struggling with chip production in so-called 12-nanometre technology in 2021/22, Apple was already at 5 nanometres at that time and Taiwan was heading straight for 2-nanometre production. What you need to know is that the internal structure of computer chips is measured in nanometres. The fewer nanometres, the more computing power can be accommodated on a chip. The gap between 12 and 2 nanometres is immense, especially since, in Beijing's view, Taiwan belongs to China anyway. So, this is where China has to catch up - or make the "leap" to Taiwan to bring the know-how there under its wing. Meanwhile, reaching for Taiwan would escalate the conflict with the USA, as tempting as it may be for Beijing, not only in view of its lead in chip production. However, in March 2022, China's National People's Congress once again confirmed Taiwan's annexation to be a key goal.[163]

China's march into the future is diametrically opposed to the self-focus in Europe. While the countries of Europe are concerned about the consequences of migration, striving to stabilise the European monetary system or worrying about the environment and the climate, China is focusing on artificial intelligence, the internet of things, robotics and space travel – all areas in which Europe has at best political announcements to show but which have not been implemented. In Germany, fast internet has been in demand almost since the internet even existed; dead spots are part of everyday life in the world's fourth largest economy. Following the diesel disaster and the shift to autonomous cars with new drive systems, Germany as a car nation has experienced an upheaval, the outcome of which is extremely uncertain. When the German government announces that it will invest three billion euros in artificial intelligence by 2025, it is tantamount to the proverbial drop in the ocean.

If Europe is not on the alert, it will end up in the future where China already sees the continent today: as a technological museum offering curious insights into times long past. China and the USA, on the other hand, are in dispute about the future – whereby China is betting on a future that is often far from desirable for Europe, as the example of Social Scoring shows. This "social assessment" is basically a modern version of the former "Stasi", i.e. "state security", in the former German Democratic Republic, as communist East Germany. Whereas back then "unofficial collaborators" were recruited to spy on their fellow human beings, in Social Scoring the surveillance takes place through modern technology. The aim then and now is to encourage people to be loyal to the state and to put a stop to excessive individualism.

Social Scoring for a better population

China is a pioneer in state surveillance in the worst sense. Since 2020, there is a so-called Social Scoring, a comprehensive digital system for assessing behaviour. All digital conduct – search queries, online reading, shopping, travelling, comments on social networks and much more – is analysed and evaluated in a point system. The more compliant the citizen is with the state, the higher their score becomes. Social scores increasingly have a direct impact on everyone's life in China: The higher the score, the greater the professional career and the more fulfilling is their private life. Depending on the scores, you get a job, a seat on a train or plane, can get a driver's licence or even get preference on online dating sites. Social Scoring does not only consider the information you provide yourself, for example in social networks. Instead, the Chinese plan relies on seamless video surveillance of the population with comprehensive recording of people, for example through facial recognition, and automatic behavioural analysis and evaluation using artificial intelligence. This plan also includes the introduction of a digital currency that can be controlled and managed better than all cash.

China takes the lead in cryptocurrencies

In the summer of 2019, the Chinese central bank PBOC startled the financial world with the announcement of a groundbreaking innovation: the "e-yuan". The term stands for a state-owned digital currency of the People's Republic of China. It would be an answer to the Bitcoin but above all to future digital currencies of the Western world – the EU, however, did not officially introduce the digital euro until 2021. By the time this book was published, the USA had not yet announced its own digital currency – why should it, as long as the "real dollar" is still "the global currency". But it is precisely this "dollar monopoly" that ultimately stands in the way of China's ascent. The fear of the US dollar being transferred to the digital world of cryptocurrencies may also have prompted the Chinese PBOC to surprisingly announce as early as 2019 that the central bank's digital currency may be considered "almost ready". With this, China seemed to be the world leader: Until then, no other country had its own cryptocurrency to present.

A national digital currency is an extremely powerful instrument – especially for the state. The Chinese government's first step seems to be to take cash out of circulation, the official reason being protection against fraud. In fact, the cash in circulation is comparatively easy to counterfeit and counterfeit money is an immense problem in China. Anyone who wants to pay with a 100-yuan banknote, which is equivalent to about 13 euros and is the largest note in China, is often subjected to a quick check. Against this background, it can be assumed that the Chinese central bank will initially focus on the private sector with the digital currency. In the long term, the cryptocurrency could be expanded to wholesale business and the capital market.

It has long been speculated whether China will introduce the e-yuan before 2025. In 2020, it became clear that in the middle of the biggest global crisis, the Chinese central bank CBDC gave permission for the national Chinese cryptocurrency, which has been successively rolled out ever since. The digital central bank currency of the People's Republic was first used in April 2020 only in the Xiangcheng district of Suzhou to pay salaries to government officials. Since May 2020, the disbursements have been successively expanded. The Bank of China, China Construction Bank, Industrial and Commercial Bank of China and Agricultural Bank of China worked closely together on the project. The Chinese payment service Alipay is responsible for the technological execution of this initial implementation. The digital central bank currency is both traceable and encryptable. Furthermore, the associated digital wallets can be designed according to the type of application. This greatly facilitates monitoring with regard to financial risks.[164]

The Chinese digital currency is already a reality as this book goes to press. The main rationale behind this – apart from the unconditional desire to nip US dominance of digital currencies in the bud at all costs – is probably the transparency that a state-controlled cryptocurrency would imply. Tax evasion, money laundering, politically undesirable financing – state control would be so comprehensive that such offences would be immediately exposed.

What sounds rather daunting from a German perspective is basically nothing new for the Chinese population. For a long time, technology companies such as Tencent via the digital all-round service WeChat and Alibaba via Alipay have been collecting masses of data on consumer behaviour. The Chinese central bank was probably more concerned with the macroeconomic fine-tuning of the economy in addition to the detection or prevention of crimes. The advantages of a digital central bank currency, however, are manifold: better availability, faster payment processing at lower costs and better monitoring of capital flows. For example, the central bank could restrict or impose higher costs on certain transactions, such as in the real estate sector, in order to avoid a bubble. Moreover, the central bank would be informed on a daily basis about capital flows between banks and shadow banks, which currently occurs, if at all, only with a considerable time lag. A digital currency would accommodate the desire of many Chinese to transfer foreign currency abroad, which would be much easier to control and, if necessary, to prevent. Moreover, in the long term, the level of automation in the industry could benefit from programmable money.

Yet the model, if it were to materialise, would go much further. In theory, a digital currency would facilitate real-time monitoring of all transactions in an economy. Combined with artificial intelligence, which also draws conclusions from the transactions in real time, this is tantamount to total monitoring of the financial system and the financial behaviour of every individual. This fits in well with China's policy of becoming the technological leader in as many strategic areas as possible and using this dominance to firstly control the domestic population and secondly successively expand the country's geostrategic role.

To implement this strategy, China is willing to invest in modern technologies on an almost unimaginable scale. But a digital currency based solely on blockchain technology, the usual process for cryptocurrencies to produce digital money, is hardly conceivable even for China in the foreseeable future. No computing factory, no matter how large, would be able to technically manage the enormous number of transactions with blockchain. For the retail sector alone, such a system would have to process around 300,000 transactions per second – before 2030, such a dimension is still considered impossible. But China will do its utmost to introduce a national digital currency as quickly as possible. A distributed strategy could serve this purpose, in which the Chinese central bank issues and guarantees digital currency, while commercial banks and other payment service providers manage the balances on behalf of the central bank. The start in 2020 in initially one city district (Xiangcheng) in the district-free city of Xiangyanm, which is rather small by Chinese standards with around half a million inhabitants, gives an indication of this distributed strategy.[165]

The world owes China six trillion dollars

A 2019 joint study by Harvard University and the Kiel Institute for the World Economy concluded that the People's Republic of China's foreign claims are around six trillion. That is about 50 percent more than the official statistics show. Almost everywhere in the world, infrastructure projects, including power plants, pipelines, bridges, tunnels, roads, railway lines, dams, schools, hospitals or satellites, are being built with Chinese billions. After the shock caused by the Lehman Brothers bankruptcy in the USA, which unleashed repercussions all over the world, the immense volume of investment from China has considerably mitigated the last fiscal crisis. But they are all loans that come from China, so the states will have to repay the sum with compound interest in the future. This is precisely what is driving more and more countries into a dangerous dependence on China - dangerous for the countries but also for China when it comes to defaults. The danger of a renewed global debt crisis as a result of the Chinese credit bubble is self-evident. Back in 2019, a group of US senators warned then US Secretary of State Mike Pompeo that Beijing was taking parts of the world "financially hostage". According to the Harvard/Kiel study, 152 states (!) are bound to China by nearly 5,000 loans and aid payments, which together add up to the aforementioned six trillion dollars.

The fear of Chinese influence via loans is also related to the fact that there is practically no transparency about China's economic management. The Western-dominated financial institutions such as the World Bank or the International Monetary Fund (IMF) are only incompletely informed. Beijing prefers to rely on its own China Development Bank (CDB) and the Export-Import Bank of China (Exim) to advance its global ambitions. Neither the CDB nor the Exim are multilateral banks but are under the exclusive control of the Chinese government and thus serve only China's political interests. This includes, for example, the financing of the New Silk Road with a global network of roads, railway lines, ports and pipelines, all of which ultimately lead to China. In a figurative sense, this often also applies to investment funds. In many cases, Beijing ensures that the loans granted to the recipient countries flow directly to Chinese contractors who build the infrastructure. This creates a closed financial circuit without involving a foreign account. In addition, the lender is always updated on the progress of construction. The study by Harvard University and the Kiel Institute for the World Economy says China has created a new form of development aid in which "state donors extend loans on commercial terms". Authors Henry Sanderson and Michael Forsythe wrote in their book "China's Superbank" for the CDB: "If the Communist Party is God, then the CDB is its prophet, extending the power of the Chinese state around the globe and cementing its power at home." One may easily classify this analysis as apt.

It is interesting to take a look at the credit agreements of the People's Republic, with which China protects itself against payment defaults. This shows that it is by no means only about good yields but about power. In many contracts, China secures direct access to raw materials, food or the profits of state-owned companies in debtor countries in the event of default. The concept is clear: either Beijing earns well from the respective loan deal or gains direct influence over a valuable resource. This Chinese strategy is light years away from the development aid understanding of Western countries. There are already quite a few examples of how well this approach works for China and how devastating it is for the countries that rely on Chinese money. In Ecuador, for example, Beijing has secured 80 per cent (!) of oil revenues to offset the cost of a huge dam. In Sri Lanka, China took over an entire port after the island nation had difficulties servicing its debt to China. As this book goes to press, there are numerous other similar cases. It is feared that Beijing will take over the state-owned energy suppliers in South Africa (Eskom) or Zambia (ZESCO).

The camouflage tactics with which the Chinese government is trying to disguise its actions lead to the conclusion that, just as with the Silk Road, it is by no means all about economic motives, but primarily about expanding China's political influence globally. Thus, "development aid" often does not go to the central bank of the recipient countries in the first place but directly to the state-owned companies there. As a result, the payment flows do not even appear in the official financial statistics of the countries. The consequence: Neither the governments of the Western countries nor the international organisations even get to know about the covert loans.

"Development dictatorship" as a model of success

One may feel reminded of the actions of the big banks in the 1970s. At that time, banks mainly from the USA but also from Europe and Japan, lent billions to resource rich countries in Latin America and Africa, often under the radar of international regulators and at high interest rates. Later, prices for mineral resources collapsed, countries could no longer service the loans and large parts of the developing world fell into a debt crisis from which they did not recover for years. One may assume that the big banks were primarily concerned with profits back then but today's China is concerned with more, namely the systematic strengthening of its geopolitical influence. The fear is a déjà-vu of the situation that prevailed in the late 1970s and 1980s. In many developing countries, the mountains of debt are as high in the 2020s as they were then. There are already unmistakable danger signals coming from some countries: Pakistan has applied for an emergency loan from the IMF, and Sierra Leone has stopped the construction of an airport that Beijing wanted to finance. But it could be too late, as the example of Africa shows, either impressively or frighteningly depending on your viewpoint.

For decades, Africa was perceived from a European and US perspective primarily as a continent of poverty, disasters and horror. Helping the people of Africa was the West's top political goal. A wave of African migration to Europe, which has intensified since 2015, was thought to reflect the poor living conditions in Africa and the political slogan was: We have to improve the situation in the countries of origin in order to stop the barely controllable migration flows. Long before that, China took a completely different view of Africa, namely as a continent with enormous development potential. Beijing provided African autocrats and dictators with sufficient financial resources so that they could cultivate their personal style of luxury and develop their country at the same time. Rwanda's President Paul Kagame spoke for a host of African potentates when he said Beijing was providing exactly what

Africa needed. For the ruling African politicians, China was a pleasant partner. The money flowed without the moral lectures that are characteristic of the West. Human rights, minimum labour standards, environmental protection or democratic principles were not considerations for receiving Chinese money – nor were bribes considerations for politicians.

The Chinese success model of a development dictatorship took a foothold in large parts of Africa. Beijing gave the money to build roads, airports, railways, industrial parks and dams and in return secured access to mineral resources and African markets. One can certainly speak of a new form of colonialism made by China. Some African countries are so heavily in debt that China could basically take over the country. This applies, for example, to the small state of Djibouti, which owes almost 70 per cent of its economic output to Beijing. In the Republic of Congo, the share is almost 30 per cent, in Kenya over 15 per cent.

Yet it is too easy to dismiss this approach as unethical, although this categorisation is irrelevant in the geopolitical power poker anyway. The local people often benefited more from this kind of "massive development aid" than from the rather trickling development funds from the West. In a survey conducted by Afrobarometer in 36 African countries, 63 per cent of respondents rated China's engagement in their countries positively.[166]

Tripartite war

No country other than the USA has spent as much money on armaments in recent years as China. Since 1990, China has accounted for 60 per cent of global growth in military spending.

In the military comparison as of 2020, the United States came out on top – but for how much longer? Admittedly, China has the upper hand with two million soldiers, compared to 1.3 million US soldiers in terms of infantry. With well over 300 operational warships – a hundred of which were built within the last ten years – China is quantitatively superior to the US fleet of around 280 ships, yet the US Navy is still considered militarily superior. In the case of submarines (China: 62, USA: 68), one might still regard them as being on par. But only four of the Chinese submarines are armed with nuclear weapons compared to 14 nuclear submarines of the Americans. Military superiority is even clearer when it comes to aircraft carriers: the USA can boast eleven, while China has just two. However, others are in the planning stage, which, just like the US carriers, will also be equipped with nuclear marine propulsion. China's maritime rearmament is strongly associated with its military doctrine, the aim being to still have enough power for a devastating counterattack in the event of a nuclear first strike by the USA, for example. But so far, China's nuclear weapons are mainly installed on land-based launching bases, which are considered relatively easy to detect and destroy with the help of modern guided weapons. Just like the Americans, Beijing therefore aims to station a substantial part of its nuclear firepower on nuclear-powered submarines, which offer the best protection even against such a powerful adversary as the USA.

Beijing is also focusing on a massive rearmament of its air force. In November 2018, a fighter aircraft with so-called thrust vectoring control was launched for the first time; this makes the Chinese jets similarly manoeuvrable to modern military aircraft from the West. China has had its first stealth jet since 2017. A stealth bomber that can rival the US B-2 bomber is scheduled to enter service in 2025.

Above all, China has invested heavily in the modernisation of its missile arsenal in recent years. China already possesses more ballistic missiles than any other state. A good half of these are medium-range ballistic missiles such as the DF-21 and DF-26 anti-ship missiles. These are called "carrier killers" in military jargon because they are able to neutralise the hitherto almost unassailable US aircraft carriers.

In these military trade-offs, it is of course not enough to simply compare China and the USA. Russia may not play a significant role in the world in terms of economy and technology but it does in military terms. The West would be well advised not to prepare for a duel but for a tripartite war.

US soldiers expect war soon

A Military Times survey revealed back in October 2018 that cyberterrorism, Russia and China were the biggest threats to US soldiers. According to the survey, almost half of the US armed forces expected their country to be involved in a new major war soon. The soldiers assessed the global situation as so unstable that a war with Russia or with China was possible in the 2020s. The year before, this share had been just five per cent. So, since 2018, the international situation has been coming to a head in the eyes of the US military. The 2020/21 pandemic has further exacerbated the conflict between China and the USA.

The US forces apparently assumed a "regular war", i.e. state against state, with China and Russia as the primary bogeymen. For example, 71 per cent of respondents saw Russia as a national security threat to the US from 2019, up 18 percentage points from the previous year, and 69 per cent saw China, up 24 points from the year before.

However, this was in clear contrast to the experiences and expectations of the previous years, which were mainly characterised by asymmetric wars and wars against "rogue states" such as North Korea or Iran. Incidentally, according to the survey conducted in the 2020s, North Korea and Iran, respectively, regarded 46 and 40 per cent of US soldiers as a threat. As recently as 2017, North Korea ranked first with 72 per cent.

The increased threat of war resulted directly from US President Donald Trump's war rhetoric during his 2016 to 2020 term. He had not only unmistakably threatened North Korea with nuclear war but had directly launched an attack in Syria, risking a military conflict with Russia. In the event that poison gas were to be used in the Syrian Idlib Governorate, the United States, together with France and the United Kingdom, threatened an offensive. The three UN veto powers were "determined to act strongly and swiftly should the Assad regime use these weapons again in the future" as in the poison gas attack on Ghouta near Damascus on

21 August 2013.[167] Mexico warned the then US president that the military would be deployed and had troops moved to the Mexican border if the country did not stop immigration to the US.

At 89 per cent, the soldiers rated the threat of cyberterrorism as even more threatening than conventional wars. However, they saw the US as poorly equipped against attacks via the Internet. Only 13 per cent of the soldiers were behind the state's defensive measures, a third simply rejected the efforts to combat cyberterrorism.[168]

US President Joe Biden clearly stated in July 2021: "I think that if we end up in a war – a real shooting war with a major power – it's going to be as a consequence of a cyber breach of great consequence. And the probability is increasing exponentially". [169] This was almost a declaration of war against either China, Russia or North Korea – the three leading anti-US cyber war nations in the world.

The USA falls behind militarily

As early as November 2018, the report of a bipartisan commission to the US Congress became public, causing horror among US politicians. In essence, the paper came to the realisation that the United States of America is on the way to losing its military edge over other major powers. There was no guarantee that the USA would win a war against China or Russia in any case. According to the report, both China and Russia continue to massively rearm; worse yet, the arms measures of both countries were apparently directly targeted against the USA.

Kathleen H. Hicks, a former Pentagon adviser under the Obama administration and a member of the Commission, blatantly warned against the complacent feeling that "the US could achieve anything they wanted around the world, including militarily". Indeed, this has been the US claim not only since Donald Trump's tenure in the Oval Office. In 2018, the year of the report, the US spent a remarkable $716 billion on this, four times more than China and ten times more than Russia.[170]

So, the arms race has been in full swing for a long time – and it will probably accelerate further under US President Joe Biden. In fact, in 2016, US President Trump already wanted to massively curtail defence spending to finance the tax cuts promised to the electorate from the savings. He wanted to impose the balance on the other NATO member states, whose clear reluctance to finance the joint military alliance had been a thorn in the side of the USA ever since US President Barack Obama' tenure of office.

China's military doctrine: Western Pacific

Unlike the United States of America, China is not aiming at military control of the entire world but at keeping potential opponents at a distance from its own country as far as possible. This includes, in particular, control of the Western Pacific, which China increasingly regards as its sea. This defensive strategy is at the core of China's military doctrine. To this end, China declared an airspace surveillance zone over the East China Sea in 2013 and turned numerous islands in the South China Sea into militarised armed bases.

There is a clearly defined military reason for this. China's current submarines, even the most modern nuclear-powered ones, are simply too noisy in operation and can therefore be too easily located and destroyed by the enemy with sonar systems. Meanwhile, for the development of more silent nuclear submarines, China needs a maritime shelter for testing purposes – and that is exactly what the East and South China Seas are for. For this very reason, Beijing has turned a number of islands in the South China Sea into fortresses and defends itself against any intrusion by foreign warships.

But the US is not willing to stand idly by and watch this increasing militarisation in the Western Pacific. In response, US President Barack Obama had already ordered a "pivot to Asia" in 2011. Under his leadership, 60 per cent of US naval forces were stationed in the Pacific instead of only 50 per cent as before. In addition, new US military bases have been established in the region. Obama's successor in the office of US president consistently continued this military strategy. This includes a second aircraft carrier permanently underway in the Pacific, as well as the increase of the US Navy from 283 (2018) to 355 ships. High-ranking US military officials doubt, however, whether this would be enough in the event of a disaster. Admiral Philip Davidson, commander of US forces in the Pacific, had to admit that Beijing controls the South China Sea "in all scenarios except a war with the US". A commission appointed by the US Congress concluded that even in the event of war, victory for the United States of America is no longer certain: "The US military could suffer unacceptably high losses in its next conflict. It could have difficulty winning a war against China or Russia, or perhaps even lose it. The US is particularly at risk should its troops be forced to fight on two fronts simultaneously." An alliance between Moscow and Beijing could thus mean the collapse of the USA as a world power. Although Russia and China have been distrustful to hostile towards each other for many years, both are united in their strict rejection of the USA as a kind of "global government". In September 2018, China and Russia undertook a major joint land and sea manoeuvre in Northeast Asia for the first time. So, it seems quite conceivable that the US could indeed become embroiled in a two-front war, the outcome of which is uncertain. That would probably be the Third World War, in this constellation, by the way, the first world war outside Europe, possibly even without European participation. By then, Europe's role could be so insignificant on a global scale that a European army would only be concerned with protecting its own external borders. This presupposes, of course, that Europe has not disintegrated into its individual states by then and that it has a European armed force at all. At the same time, it would probably mean Europe's withdrawal from NATO with the USA. And the extent to which Europe can remain out of a Third World War depends, of course, on the state of the American nuclear weapons and other missiles on European soil by then.

However, all this only represents the military view. But in today's globalised world, nations, economic and power-political considerations are closely interconnected. A trade war instigated by the US would hit China's export position massively but at the same time it would shake the US capital market just as badly. In the nuclear age, mutual destruction was considered ultima ratio: the aggressor with nuclear weapons had to assume that it would be equally devastated by the nation attacked.

This "mutually assured destruction" of the past has taken on a new economic form today. While in the Cold War of the Free World against the Soviet Union it was primarily the military arms race that decided victory and defeat, nowadays other components have emerged: economic potency and technological superiority or inferiority. In both fields, China is making every effort to compete with the US.

USA arms Taiwan against China

The United States' military deal with Taiwan in the summer of 2019 seemed like a resounding slap in the face to China: the U.S. sold 66 F-16 fighter jets to Taiwan. The arms deal, worth a total of eight billion dollars (equivalent to 7.2 billion euros), included 75 engines and other systems in addition to the fighter jets. The US government classified the multi-billion-dollar military deal as in line with the "historic relationship" between the US and China, while China called it a "serious violation" of agreements and a "serious interference in China's internal affairs". After all, Beijing regards the island state of Taiwan as a renegade province that will one day be reunited with the mainland - by military force if necessary. The military support by the USA could therefore only be understood as a provocation – but was no longer big news in 2019. Taiwan had already acquired an F-16 fleet in 1992 and has modernised it several times over the years.

Hypothetical attack on Europe

For a hypothetical attack on a European country, by the way, military strategists rely on a combination of precision missiles, cyber-attacks and social media. The aim would be to simply disrupt the everyday life of the population. If the supply of electricity, water, Internet and food is disrupted, every European country would be considered defeated without a single soldier having to march in.

If fear and panic were incited via the social media, surrender would be considered certain within two weeks.[171] The 2020 pandemic has indeed proven that even comparatively simple restrictions in everyday life can turn the population against its own government. The threat alone would probably be enough to drive the predictable world of the West to the brink of the abyss.

This is exactly what happened with the invasion of Ukraine by Russian troops in 2022. It was a vicious conventional military attack that could hardly be surpassed in brutality. While the old post-war world order, in which the USA was the protecting power for Europe, seemed to be coming to an end, the Western defence alliance experienced a renaissance in the face of Russian aggression in 2022. The roots go back to the time after the Second World War.

The West fights back: NATO

The fate of Europe after the Second World War was intricately related to that of the United States of America. The difference in development between the Federal Republic of Germany and the then German Democratic Republic made it clear for decades why it was more desirable for people to live in the free West according to the American way of life instead of in the communist East under the Soviet heel of Russia. The division of Germany typified the division of the world into the West and the Eastern Bloc.

Against this background, the Western military alliance of the North Atlantic Treaty Organisation (NATO) was launched under Article 51 of the UN Charter. The military-political pact was created after the Second World War as a defence system against the Soviet Union and the Eastern Bloc. On 4 April 1949, Belgium, Denmark, France, the United Kingdom, Iceland, Italy, Luxembourg, the Netherlands, Norway, Portugal, Canada and the USA signed the North Atlantic Treaty, which came into force on 24 August 1949.

NATO's zigzag course

NATO's objectives and strategy have changed fundamentally several times since then; one could also speak of a zigzag course. Initially, the strategy of containment laid down on 6 January 1950 applied, i.e. defence against a Soviet attack on the Alliance territory as far east as possible. The outbreak of the Korean War in June 1950, in which China also intervened in November 1950, led to a massive rearmament in Europe because people feared a Soviet attack. On 24 October 1950, France forged ahead: The then French Prime Minister René Pleven put forward the proposal of a European Army, led by a European Defence Minister. Only shortly after, on 20 December 1950, the member states of the Brussels Pact – also called the Western Union – decided to incorporate the previous military organisation into NATO.

The Brussels Pact was concluded on 17 March 1948 by France, the United Kingdom, Belgium, Luxembourg and the Netherlands as a military alliance and merged in 1954 into the Western European Union, which also included the Federal Republic of Germany, newly formed after the Second World War. The aim was to pool the severely depleted military capacities in Western Europe to be prepared for a possible attack by the Soviet Union. By joining forces with NATO on 20 December 1950, Western Europe and North America became militarily "one heart and one soul" – until 2018, when France's head of state Emmanuel Macron put a European army on the political agenda for the first time, also with an eye on the United States of America.

In the meantime, however, there have been several changes of strategy in NATO, including the plan to destroy at least half the world in the event of an attack by the Soviet Union. The USA had developed this nuclear strategy of massive retaliation, which envisaged responding to an attack on a NATO state of any kind with a devastating nuclear counterattack. On 21 March 1953, NATO adopted this strategy in the "Overall Strategic Concept for the Defence of the North Atlantic Treaty Organisation".

The arms race between the Western and Eastern blocs began. In response to Germany's accession to NATO on 9 May 1955, the Soviet Union founded the Warsaw Pact just five days later as the Eastern Bloc's military assistance pact and a counterweight to NATO. On 13 On 13 March 1957, the USA announced that it would equip its armed forces with nuclear weapons. On 12 October 1960, NATO Supreme Allied Commander General Lauris Norstad officially proposed to NATO the establishment of a multilateral nuclear force. The USA then launched its first Minuteman intercontinental ballistic missile from a bunkered silo on 30 January 1961.

On 10 May 1961, US President John F. Kennedy stressed to the NATO Military Committee the strengthening of conventional combat power and the need to control nuclear weapons. The stationing of Soviet medium-range ballistic missiles in Cuba led to the Cuban Missile Crisis in October 1962. The world was on the brink of war. Never had nuclear war been as likely as it was at that time.

Against this background, France's President Charles de Gaulle began to build up his own nuclear forces, the "*Force de frappe,*" from 1958 onwards, which were to act completely independently of the USA. With the first French nuclear explosion on 13 February 1960, France entered the circle of nuclear powers. Charles de Gaulle demanded that all US and Canadian units stationed in France be placed under French command and, after the US refused, called for the withdrawal of all foreign forces and NATO headquarters from France on 10 February 1966, and declared the withdrawal of French troops from NATO. So, France already distanced itself from NATO under Charles de Gaulle, albeit as a solo effort, while in 2018 Emmanuel Macron apparently wanted to put France on a military footing together with the other European countries, detached from the US but in alliance with its European neighbours.

After the strategy of massive retaliation in the Cuban Missile Crisis of 1962 had almost led to a nuclear catastrophe – in other words, to World War III in one stroke – on 14 December 1967 NATO adopted the strategy of Flexible Response, which applied until the end of the Cold War. Instead of threatening to wipe out the world in the event of an attack, a moderate defensive strategy adapted to the situation applied from then on. Moreover, NATO relied on a two-pillar system, which was to ensure military security through conventional and the then newly developed tactical nuclear weapons on the one hand, and a policy of détente on the other.

As early as 1970, the question of greater financial participation by European NATO partners in the defence alliance arose, and US President Trump raised it with renewed topicality in 2016. At that time, the Euro Group, the group of Europeans in NATO, had adopted a "Defence Improvement Programme" on 2 December 1970 at a cost of 420 million dollars. On 12 On 12 December 1979, the infamous NATO Double-Track Decision was made: NATO announced the deployment of new medium-range ballistic missiles and cruise missiles armed with nuclear warheads and at the same time demanded bilateral negotiations between the superpowers USA and USSR on the limitation of their intermediate-range nuclear missiles – the Intermediate Nuclear Forces, INF – with a range of between 1,000 and 5,500 km in Europe. Nuclear armament and arms control were to complement each other.

Then the age of perestroika dawned, the transformation of the social, political and economic system of the Soviet Union under Mikhail Gorbachev, General Secretary of the Central Committee of the Communist Party of the Soviet Union (CPSU) from March 1985, which ruled the USSR and thus the entire Eastern Bloc. Since then, the Soviet Union offered far-reaching nuclear disarmament. In 1987, the USA and the USSR agreed in the INF Treaty to withdraw, destroy and ban the production of all their ammunition-guided missiles with ranges of 500 to 5,500 km and their carrier systems. As far as we know, both countries fulfilled this obligation by May 1991 – when the US government announced in autumn 2018 that it would terminate the INF Treaty and start a new arms race.[172]

In 1989, the Iron Curtain fell, the Eastern Bloc gradually dissolved and the geopolitical situation in Europe changed fundamentally. The Warsaw Pact as NATO's arch-enemy military alliance disappeared, and a new concept was needed. Finally, on 8 November 1991, the previous "Flexible Response" was replaced by a new strategy of dialogue, cooperation and maintenance of defence capability. The alliance also offered itself to the UN as a military alliance for use in peacekeeping operations. This was matched by NATO's readiness for out-of-area missions, i.e. also outside the territory of NATO countries, which was agreed in 1992. Since then, NATO missions have been possible anywhere in the world after authorisation by the UN Security Council. Examples of this were the second Gulf War against Iraq in 1991, in which a number of NATO countries took part under the leadership of the USA and with the participation of other countries, and the air strikes against Serbian positions in Bosnia-Herzegovina in 1994/95. In both cases, it became abundantly clear that the military factor as a concrete mandate for action in international politics had gained massive importance after the Cold War.

In the process, NATO took on regulatory tasks, sometimes by military means, which would have been better suited to the UN. The dissolution of former Yugoslavia was a case in point: while the West's military conflict settlement was primarily aimed at maintaining the structures that existed at the time, various population groups saw it as an opportunity to realise their ideas of their own states. Albania, Kosovo, Serbia, Croatia, Bosnia, Herzegovina, Macedonia – the great Eastern European civil war would presumably have been unavoidable but NATO's intervention certainly did not contribute to pacification. March 1999,

NATO began air strikes against Belgrade as part of the Kosovo war.

It was the first NATO operation outside an alliance case, and the first NATO military strike without an explicit UN mandate. It marked the beginning of a new era in which NATO gained massive importance as the military arm of politics.[173]

Nine-Eleven – the first case of alliance

The terrorist attacks of 11 September 2001 shook the world. Immediately afterwards, for the first time in its history, NATO provisionally fully enforced the case for alliance under Article 5 of the NATO Treaty, on 1 October. This Article 5 stipulates that an armed attack on an Ally, in this case the USA, is deemed to be an attack on all NATO countries. The goal stated is to restore and maintain the security of the North Atlantic area. So, if another state had attacked the USA, an immediate counterattack would probably have been the result. However, in 2001 there was no state aggressor, no declaration of war, not even a clear perpetrator. To be sure, the Allies provided intelligence support and granted US forces overflight rights and access to airfields, ports and other facilities. In addition, Operation Active Endeavour was launched on 26 October 2001 with the aim of maritime surveillance to record and document civilian maritime traffic. But ultimately, the views of NATO partners on how to proceed in the aftermath of the terror of 11 September 2001 diverged widely. The fundamental question arose as to how NATO should respond to an attack by a few terrorists.

As the attackers of 9/11 were believed to be the Afghan-based terrorist organisation Al-Qaeda, and the Afghan-based Taliban refused to take action against them, a US-led military coalition intervened in October 2001, ushering in a new phase of direct foreign involvement in the Afghan civil war with the deployment of NATO troops. Once again, it became clear that NATO was taking on an increasingly regulatory role, i.e. serving to enforce policies desired by Western governments by military means.

This development continued with the International Security Assistance Force (ISAF), which fulfilled a security and reconstruction mission in Afghanistan from 2001 to 2014. After initially being jointly led by several European countries, ISAF came under NATO command with the approval of the UN Security Council. However, it was not a UN Blue Helmet mission but remained a so-called peace enforcement operation under the responsibility of the participating states.

In both Eastern Europe and Afghanistan, it became clear that NATO was increasingly engaged in so-called state building, with and without a UN mandate. The US administration of President Joe Biden and Vice President Kamala Harris, installed in 2021, is undoubtedly narrowing the gap between the US and Europe in many ways, including with regard to NATO.

However, the severe defeat of the United States in Afghanistan in 2021, in which the US left its European allies alone almost overnight, put the transatlantic alliance to a severe test. For more than 20 years, Europe and the USA had jointly tried to transform Afghanistan into a Western-style state. But in 2021, the newly elected US President Joe Biden gave up. And it turned out: Once the USA started its withdrawal, nothing remained of the 20-year effort.

In 2001, America's revenge for the 9/11 attacks began. Twenty years later, the Taliban set out to avenge their expulsion from power and tried to wipe out everything that had emerged in between. As late as July 2021, US President Joe Biden declared: "The likelihood there's going to be the Taliban overrunning everything and owning the whole country is highly unlikely". One month later, in August 2021, this was exactly the case. The Afghan head of government, Ashran Ghani, installed by the Western states, fled head over heels abroad, the Afghan army trained by the West almost completely deserted and the Taliban overtook the entire country within a few weeks. It was an unconditional surrender.

The Taliban takeover in the summer of 2021 happened so rapidly that neither the Americans nor their Western allies had enough time for an orderly withdrawal – not even of their diplomatic staff, and certainly not for the supporters on the ground, the so-called local forces, local volunteers in building democracy according to the Western model, who had the most to fear from the Taliban. TV pictures of hundreds of them trying to get onto a plane via a rickety gangway with not even enough room for a fraction of the crowd went around the world. Other footage showed desperate people walking on the runway next to a US military aircraft, some clinging to the wheel arches. Horrific images documented how people fell from a plane that was already airborne.[174]

"With thirteen thousand their trail they began. Only one man came home from Afghanistan". Theodor Fontane already wrote about the devastating defeat of the British Empire in Afghanistan.[175] Like the British and the Soviets, the Americans later suffered the same fate.

Afghanistan 2021 was like Saigon 1975

The international community's involvement in Afghanistan ended in 2021 after twenty years of chaos. The scene looked worse than the US withdrawal from Saigon in 1975 during the retreat from Vietnam. Thousands of people were desperately waiting to be flown out of Afghanistan via the airlift of the Americans, British, Canadians, Indians and other countries in August 2021. The British Defence Minister Ben Wallace admitted in front of the cameras with tear-filled eyes: "Some people will be left behind".[176].

The US Inspector General for Afghanistan Reconstruction attested his government numerous wrong decisions due to "complete ignorance" of the situation in Afghanistan – not only at the time of the troop withdrawal in 2021 but already 20 years earlier. The US government had wrongly assumed that the governance challenges in Iraq and Afghanistan were similar. "In fact, they were not", says an Inspector General's report. The misjudgement of the social and political environment in Afghanistan by the US government resulted in many initiatives for the stabilisation and reconstruction of the country being inadequately adapted to local conditions.[177]

Wolfgang Ischinger, former German ambassador in London and Washington and head of the Munich Security Conference since 2008, analysed: "The case of Afghanistan manifests the current debility of the West in geostrategic terms. Westlessness?

This does not bode well for other conflict zones and will tend to empower undemocratic currents. That is why Afghanistan is a litmus test for the ability of the entire international community of states to settle conflicts. In Syria, in Yemen, in Libya, it has not demonstrated crisis prevention and crisis management, to say the least. It would send a pathetic signal if the United Nations were to fail again in Afghanistan" [178]

It was a polite analysis; in fact, there is no denying that the international community, and with it the UN, has failed miserably in Afghanistan. Following the USA's desire for revenge after the attacks of 11 September 2001, practically all Western nations had embarked on a deadly adventure in Afghanistan. But they should have known better. After all, the Soviet intervention in Afghanistan between 1979 and 1989 had already failed miserably. This began with the Soviet Union's military support of the Afghan rulers, who had come to power in a coup against the numerous groups of holy warriors, the Mujahideen, who formed primarily as a reaction to the secularisation of Afghanistan.[179] However, instead of supporting the liberal tendencies in the country, the Islamist rebel groups were supported politically and materially by the USA as well as some NATO states and parts of the Islamic world "on principle," namely the principle of confronting the Soviet Union.[180] In other words, for years, the USA and numerous Western states have themselves promoted extremist groups that later became their enemies. Certainly not only but also because of this policy, the Soviet Union of the time conceded defeat. The withdrawal of Soviet troops left Afghanistan politically and militarily in disarray.[181] In this comparison, the US withdrawal in 2021 was different: the United States left behind a Taliban state, which the terrorist organisation consequently renamed the "Islamic Emirate".[182]

It seems likely that Czech President Miloš Zeman who sharply criticised the withdrawal of the USA and NATO from Afghanistan will be proven right: under the Taliban, the country will become a "centre of terrorism". Promptly, on the twentieth anniversary of the Nine-Eleven attacks in the USA, the Al-Qaeda terrorist network came forward with a video message. For around 60 minutes, the successor to Osama Bin-Laden, who had been killed by the USA, called for a fight against the Western states and their allies in the Middle East. The Nine-Eleven attacks were "an injury", the like of which had never before been inflicted upon America; 20 years later, the USA left Afghanistan "broken and defeated". [183] This threat corresponds to Czech President Milos Zeman's assessment that there is a threat of Islamist terrorist attacks "basically all over the world". Zeman criticised that the withdrawal of the USA had forfeited the prestige of the world's leading power and NATO had triggered "doubts about its raison d'être". After all, one of the central tasks of the defence alliance had been to stave off international terrorism.[184]

Russia and China speak out on Afghanistan

The impact of the Afghan disaster will reach far into the 2020s and beyond – not only in Afghanistan but throughout the region, and even globally. Thus, almost simultaneously with the withdrawal of US troops in the summer of 2021, Russia declared that it had begun talks with the Taliban and hoped for good accord. While the West had always regarded the Taliban only as enemies, Russia had already been in informal talks with them for years, completely independent of any official recognition. For some time now, Russia has positioned itself as a kind of protective power for the region. Tajik, Russian and Uzbek militaries have already held joint manoeuvres. The withdrawal of the USA in 2021 was accompanied by Russia's re-entry into the region.[185] However, Moscow also saw the terrorist threat emanating from Afghanistan: "There is a danger that terrorists and various groups that have found refuge in Afghanistan will take advantage of the chaos left behind by our Western partners," said Russian President Vladimir Putin. He rightly asserts that drug smuggling and illegal migration are likely to increase – affecting not only Russia but the whole of Europe. At the same time, Moscow issued a clear warning to the USA in 2021: Russia strictly rejected the stationing of US troops in Central Asia. The rationale: any state that allows US forces in its country loses its stability.[186]

In 2021, China saw the failure of the military intervention in Afghanistan as evidence of the USA's waning power. "The fall of Kabul rings the death knell for the decline of US hegemony," gloated the Chinese state news agency Xinhua. The relationship with Afghanistan is nevertheless ambivalent for China. As much as the fortress against the USA is desired, China attaches little importance to the influence of the Muslim Taliban on the domestic population. Beijing is afraid of radical Islamism seeping into China. After all, China and Afghanistan share a 76-km border.[187]

China and Russia but also Pakistan, Iran and Turkey, tend to see the West's withdrawal as an opportunity. For Afghanistan has mineral resources worth several trillion US dollars. All these countries are hoping for lucrative contracts from the Taliban and the opportunity to exploit the country's precious raw materials.[188] Afghanistan is rich in iron, copper, lithium, rare-earth elements, and gold.[189] As the producer of almost half of all industrial goods in the world, China needs the lion's share of all raw materials. Beijing, which is the largest foreign investor in Afghanistan, is already leading the race when it comes to building an efficient mining system in Afghanistan's Hindu Kush.[190] Thus, millions and billions of products that will be bought around the globe in the future could at least indirectly contribute to increasing the Taliban's wealth.

European army faces huge hurdles

In the first half of the 2020s, the realisation emerged that Europe needed to take more care of its own security. The anti-European Trump reign from 2016 to 2020, the coronavirus pandemic of 2020/21 and the Afghanistan disaster of 2021 are likely to have served as "accelerators". Russia's invasion of Ukraine in 2022 on the one hand strengthened the NATO alliance with the USA but on the other hand also made clear how important it is for Europe to have its own robust military presence. All four events were wake-up calls to the European Union to defend its own destiny by joining forces in the truest sense of the word.

But organising a common EU defence is fraught with formidable hurdles. The mere coordination of the different weaponry in use in the nation states seems impossible; in any case, it is uneconomical. At least there are approaches such as the EU directive on arms export policy, cooperation between EU states on military projects and the European Defence Fund for financing. From there to an EU army is certainly still a long way off, driven by the aggravation of the global political situation but hampered by the European Union's internal discord.

The key question to be resolved is who makes the decision on the deployment of soldiers. Although the European Parliament lends itself to this, at the time of printing this book it does not yet have a legal basis for this. Moreover, the EU member states will hardly be able to wrest it from them that troop contingents from their countries are deployed without the authorisation of their respective national parliaments. But if all member states were to agree on the deployment of an EU army, at least some of which would have to consult their parliaments first, the soldiers would probably never get their marching orders.

The harmonisation of weapons systems is likely to be equally challenging. While the USA has exactly one type of main battle tank, Europe has seventeen different models. In terms of infantry fighting vehicles (IFV), the USA has two types, Europe 20. Fighter jets: USA six, Europe 20. Naval regattas: USA four, Europe 29. In total, the thirty main weapons systems of the USA are opposed by 178 of the Europeans. Moreover, Europe lacks ships, aircraft, aircraft carriers and even reconnaissance equipment to be able to seriously intervene in conflicts. Analysis suggests that the EU would at best manage humanitarian disaster operations on its own. This is far from its own goals of being able to prevent or even end armed conflicts in Europe and neighbouring regions.[191]

In addition, Europe's political will to actually engage in armed conflict had long since waned as a result of the Second World War. For large parts of today's population, a war of Europe or even in Europe was unthinkable – so far beyond their imagination that they did not want to prepare for it and did not intend to give a mandate to any political party that seriously wanted to conduct such a debate. The immense defence costs associated with this were counterbalanced in daily political life by the social benefits that could be achieved with these funds.

At least, that was the situation before Russia sent its soldiers, tanks, warplanes and other war equipment to Ukraine on 24 February 2022.

Against this backdrop, NATO Secretary General Jan Stoltenberg's public deliberations in 2019 about nuclear rearmament in Europe while absurd at the time, have nevertheless been within the realm of the conceivable since 2022.[192]

After all, the Brexit from the European Union in 2021 cleared the way for the EU Defence Initiative for Permanent Structured Cooperation (PESCO). This was already established in 2017 and included 46 projects at the beginning of 2021. These were based on 20 legally binding commitments by all 22 participating European member states to cooperate more closely in the planning and development of military capabilities.[193]The United Kingdom – along with Denmark and Malta – had acted as a constant hindrance before Brexit and hindered the further development of PESCO.[194] The chairman of the European People's Party (EPP), which has been the largest group in the European Parliament since 1999, Manfred Weber, promptly called for a rapid EU reaction force and a cyber defence brigade in 2021. In his view, Europe is at a turning point. And the USA is "no longer prepared to be the world's policeman". He said literally: "Belarus, Ukraine, North Africa, the Middle East – the Americans will not solve these problems for us [...] The EU should step up efforts to strengthen its own military capacity and depend less on America".[195]

When Russia invaded Ukraine in 2022, it became clear how militarily dependent Europe is on the US. For a long time, the B-52 bombers of the US Air Force had disappeared from Europe. In the spring of 2022, the "stratofortresses", as the long-range penetration bombers are also called, appeared again with increasing frequency over Germany. The B-52s were part of the so-called "Task Force Bomber Europe". The US Air Force regularly trained with flight crew and soldiers from other NATO members in order to optimise the interaction between the units. In 2022, the bombers – also called "BUFF" (*Big Ugly Fat Fucker*) in pilot jargon – were sighted not only in Germany but also in Austria, the Czech Republic and Romania, among other countries. "The rotation of the 'Bomber Task Force' gives us an excellent opportunity to integrate and train with our allies, especially during this challenging time," said General Jeff Harrigian, Commander of US Air Forces in Europe and Africa, at the beginning of March 2022. Earlier this year, the US military had moved four BUFF aircraft to the air force base at Fairford in the UK.[196] The question of whether the US government had already foreseen the war in Ukraine at that time could never be clarified.

The world is re-arming

In any case, the world has been re-arming not just since 2021 but since 2017. Global military expenditure had already risen steadily from 1999 to 2011, and between 2012 and 2016, it remained stable before increasing again as of 2017. In total, the nations of the world had military expenditure of around 1.76

trillion euros in 2019. It marked an all-time high since the Stockholm-based peace research institute SIPRI provided globally consistent comparative data for the first time.[197] In 2019, military spending around the globe increased at the fastest rate in the previous decade.[198] The US accounted for over a third of all military spending worldwide in 2019.

This was almost as much as all eight next ranking countries – China, Saudi Arabia, India, France, Russia, the United Kingdom, Germany and Japan – combined. China alone spent about as much money on the military in 2019 as the next four countries. For the 25th consecutive year, China increased its annual military spending in 2019 – with no end in sight; on the contrary, further increases are expected in the 2020s.[199]

The Stockholm-based peace research institute SIPRI warned in 2020 of a renaissance of nuclear weapons. SIPRI reported that, going into 2020, Russia had 6375 nuclear warheads, the USA had over 5800, China 320, France 290, the UK 215, Pakistan 160, India more than 150 and Israel more than 90. The researchers described the nuclear weapons programme in North Korea with thirty to forty nuclear weapons as "active but very opaque". Even more frightening in 2020 was the realisation by the Stockholm peace researchers that the nuclear powers were working on a new generation of nuclear weapons. Both Russia and the USA had initiated expensive and extensive programmes to modernise their nuclear warheads, transportable aircraft and production facilities. Moreover, nuclear weapons were again playing a more key role in their military planning for the 2020s, reversing a trend that had prevailed since the end of the Cold War. The Chinese development of a so-called nuclear triad of new sea- and land-based missiles and nuclear-capable jets was cited as an example.[200]

Not only the quantity but above all the quality of the rearmament for the 2020s is frightening. The struggle not only between China and the USA will undoubtedly be augmented by new types of weapons and new theatres of war in the 2020s.

Killer robots on the march

All superpowers have been working feverishly for years on the development of so-called "lethal autonomous weapon systems" (LAW), one can also say "killer robots".[201] These include robots that shoot around, self-guided drones, autonomous combat aircraft and who knows exactly what else is being developed in military laboratories. At its core, it is about lethal weapons that can destroy largely without human intervention through Artificial Intelligence (AI). These AI weapons are supposed to select targets independently, fire autonomously and continuously learn how to inflict the most damage on the enemy through "machine learning". "Flash war" is what the experts call the use of these soulless killer robots.

The Foreign Office of the Federal Republic of Germany described the horror scenario of the future as early as 2019 as follows: "Shooting robots, large-scale hacker attacks on power supply systems, or AI-supported novel missile systems have long since become a real danger for twenty-first century warfare. Artificial intelligence in weaponry must not lead to killer robots fighting the wars of the future without any human control whatsoever. We need an international ban on these systems". [202]

Since 2014, the United Nations has been trying to put a stop to this soulless activity. But in the 2020s, when civilian research is working hard to make cars and trucks drive autonomously, when artificial intelligence is finding its way into smartphones, homes and data clouds, it is unrealistic to expect arms manufacturers, to forego AI weapons. It would be equally illusory to believe that superpowers such as the United States, China or Russia will not spend vast sums to achieve military AI supremacy. Other states in Europe, the Middle East or Asia could be forced to rely on AI weapons as well in order not to become militarily helpless in the future. The next arms race thus seems pre-programmed. At the time of going to press, the USA, China, Israel, South Korea, Russia and the United Kingdom are already known to be massively forging ahead with the development of autonomous weapon systems.[203]

Certainly, some countries with a strong arms export business, such as the Federal Republic of Germany, will take the new killer generations into account in their future national arms control policy. Nevertheless, one does not have to be too much of a pessimist to see the danger that the killer robots could end up in the hands of terrorists.

Arms race in space

In addition to the rearmament with killer robots, another arms race is on the agenda for the 2020s, namely in space. Space has been used for military purposes since the 1950s, initially mainly by the USA and the Soviet Union.

In view of current technological developments, there is concern for the 2020s that active weapon systems will be stationed in space, for example to threaten satellites or missiles or even objects on Earth from there. That is why the UN has been calling for negotiations for years to prevent the stationing of active weapons systems in space.[204]

While the beginnings of humanity in space were mainly determined by the United States of America and the Soviet Union, China will certainly want to get involved in the 2020s. It is almost symbolic that the People's Republic of China hoisted its national flag on the moon for the first time in the first year of the new decade. The spacecraft "Chang'e 5", named after the Chinese goddess of the moon, hoisted the two-metre-wide and 90-centimetre-high Chinese flag in 2020 as part of an unmanned lunar landing.[205]

So the 2020s and 2030s are likely to see a military arms race far beyond the Cold War rearmament between 1947 and 1989. And completely new fields of armament will be acquired. In addition to outer space, this includes cyberspace, i.e. attacks via the internet.

Cyber war – the war on the Internet

US President Joe Biden seriously stated in 2021: "I think that if we end up in a war – a real shooting war with a major power – it's going to be as a consequence of a cyber breach of great consequence. And the probability is increasing exponentially".[206] The danger of a cyber war cannot be more clearly evoked.

Studies suggest that the world has entered the 2020s with around 75 billion Internet-connected devices. About 90 percent of the world's population over the age of six owned a mobile device in 2020. The global data volume was estimated to be around 50 trillion gigabytes in 2020. Smart factories, smart homes, self-driving cars – the digital revolution is in full swing and unfortunately also opens a wide range of new opportunities for criminals. This applies to criminal gangs but of course also to state criminals, for example computer hackers who are on the Internet on behalf of the state.

In fact, information systems and the infrastructures that depend on them are likely to be the most vulnerable target of all states. The mere fact that what one would assume to be the most secure agency in the world, the US National Security Agency, had millions of secret documents stolen by the employee of an external consulting firm – Booz Allen Hamilton (keyword: Snowden affair) – basically says everything about the security of state computer systems. Booz Allen Hamilton is not a hacker group but is one of the US government's leading technology consultancies, with more than 24,000 employees. With friends like these, who needs enemies?[207]

If the enemies still come into play, it becomes even more dramatic. In early 2018, Chinese hackers managed to obtain 614 gigabytes of top-secret information about the US Navy's "Sea Dragon" armament project. The attackers hacked into the poorly secured network of a company working for the Naval Undersea Warfare Center (NUWC). This is a military organisation that conducts research and development for submarines and underwater weapons. According to reports, the hackers were able to capture the top-secret plans of the new supersonic anti-ship missile "Sea Dragon", which is to provide maritime security in the 2020s. The navy certifies that the "Sea Dragon" has a "resounding offensive capability". Military experts classify them as the forerunners of a new generation of highly networked "intelligent" weaponry that could be launched from a "dumb carrier" such as a container ship.

This is possible because the new missile is not commanded from the launching ship but is integrated into a complex control system. Furthermore, "signals and sensor data, submarine information on encryption systems and electronic warfare" ended up in the hands of the cyber criminals. If the US military can protect its own projects so "well", how much do they care about preserving the data privacy of their people?

Cyber-attacks that become known are only the tip of an iceberg: most attacks, including data theft, are not even reported by companies, let alone by state institutions or even the military. The number of unreported cases is correspondingly high. In 2015, some time ago, approximately 59 million (!) cyber-attacks were detected worldwide. In 2009, there were only 3.4 million attacks. In 2020, for the first time, there had been more than one billion cyber-attacks; the economic damage exceeded the $1 trillion mark worldwide for the first time.[208]

The security problems known as "Spectre", "Meltdown" and "Foreshadow" show how deep the insecurity runs. All three cases involve serious security vulnerabilities in the microprocessors (CPU) of all major chip manufacturers such as Intel, AMD, ARM, Apple, IBM and Motorola, which allow attackers to take control of a computer's central chips. One can confidently speak of the "worst case scenario", because it was a matter of fundamental errors in chip development that went back at least to 1991 and which were simply adopted with each new processor generation. Safe processors only became available in 2019; only computers, tablets and smartphones built after 2019 can be considered safe – at least until a new fundamental flaw is detected in the processor generations of the 2020s.

Warning to the digital society

On 12 May 2017, the biggest warning to digital society to date took its course. On this Black Friday of the digital world, a global cyber-attack was launched under the name WannaCry, infecting over 230,000 computers in 150 countries. In all cases, the attackers demanded a ransom. The malware encrypted about 1,000 selected files on the computer and then demanded that the user pay a certain amount in the cryptocurrency Bitcoin within a precisely defined period; otherwise, they would suffer data loss. In addition, WannaCry tried to infect as many other computers as possible immediately after it had installed itself. The attack was described by the European law enforcement agency Europol as an unprecedented event in terms of its scale. Targets in at least 99 countries were affected.

Secret services destabilize the cyber world

In many cases, state intelligence agencies are behind the attacks or – if they do not attack – they shamelessly exploit security gaps that have been discovered to infiltrate companies and authorities in other countries with their spyware. This was also the case with WannaCry. It was a small security leak in the environment of Microsoft's Windows computer system that the US National Security Agency (NSA) discovered and used for more than five years for its own spyware before this very programme was stolen from them by foreign hackers, presumably from North Korea. If the NSA had informed the manufacturer Microsoft about the leak from the beginning, it would have been possible to close it quickly and the world's largest cyber-attack to date would never have taken place.

It is not an isolated case that the secret services keep security vulnerabilities they become aware of to themselves and exploit them instead of notifying the manufacturer for them to take remedial action. As early as 2018, Microsoft's president and chief legal officer Brad Smith referred to repeated disclosures of such spam programmes from CIA and NSA assets. He compared this to the loss of cruise missiles from military installations and accused "the governments of the world" of failing to warn against software flaws that their intelligence agencies discover. The Microsoft president argued: "We need governments to consider the damage to civilians that comes from hoarding these vulnerabilities and the use of these exploits".[209]

Attack on the vaccines

As if it needed anymore confirmation about the potential danger of cyber war, the European Medicines Agency (EMA) had to announce an "illegal access" shortly before Christmas 2020.[210] The hackers had gained access to the vaccine documents of the German company BioNTech, one of the vaccines that were supposed to make the world immune to the coronavirus. To clarify: the hackers did not obtain the information from BioNTech itself but from the responsible state licensing authority. At least the authority launched an investigation "immediately". One must imagine the situation at that time. Practically the entire world was desperately searching for vaccines against the coronavirus, the company BioNTech had finally found an effective vaccine and the European authority responsible for the approval of this vaccine was not able to sufficiently protect the documents submitted by the pharmaceutical manufacturer. It was not revealed who was behind the hacker attack but the assumption that it was a state is obvious, for example China, Russia or the USA.

As early as 2015, the German Federal Intelligence Service wrote in a classified planning document that only became known through the Snowden revelations. *Cyber-attacks pose a great threat to the environment through possible information leaks from government and business, influencing, disrupting or damaging information, communication or control systems in the public and private sectors thus posing a high threat potential and endangering Germany as a leading high-tech country and important business location. With the cyber-rearmament in numerous countries, including China and Russia, as well as criminal and terrorist players, the threats have significantly increased in professionalism and quantity. The inexorably growing "Internet of Things" has a compounding effect. Inconspicuous everyday items, such as remote-controlled light bulbs or Internet Protocol Television, can suddenly be "taken over" by a cyber-attacker and turned into digital weapons, from any corner of the globe.*

Even today, the dangers of a future digital pandemic could hardly be described with more vision. In its "Global Risk Report 2020", the World Economic Forum has identified cybercrime as the second largest security risk to the global economy by 2030. However, this is not only true for the economy but for the entire world in all its aspects. The greatest threat – ranking even higher than the cyber threat – is nuclear war. With the end of the Cold War, nuclear missiles were out of the public eye. But of course they still exist - and even more of them than ever before, as will be explained in the next chapter.

But just as nuclear power can also be used peacefully to generate energy, there are also benefits to be gained from the hacker scene.

Hacker attack on Putin

The hacker attacks against the Russian invasion of Ukraine, which, as mentioned elsewhere, started immediately after the invasion, spread faster than Putin's tanks could occupy the neighbouring country. The hackers from Anonymous had declared war on Vladimir Putin.

Within just over a week of launching the invasion, the hacker group took control of more than 2500 websites of government agencies, airports and media in Russia and Belarus. Anonymous explicitly emphasised that it did not want to harm the Russian population and therefore did not attack critical infrastructure such as nuclear power plants.

Thus, the hackers concentrated mainly on media targeting the population of Russia. Videos shown on almost all Russian TV channels said: "We are normal citizens of Russia. We are against the war on the territory of Ukraine. This war was waged by

Putin's criminal, authoritarian regime on behalf of ordinary Russian citizens. Russians, oppose the genocide in Ukraine."

On the website of the newspaper "Izvestia" this text appeared: "We urge you to stop this madness, do not send your sons and husbands to certain death. Putin makes us lie and endangers us. ... In a few years we will be living just like in North Korea. This is not our war, let's stop it!"

Nuclear war: nobody wants it, right?

The fear of a Third World War was widespread in view of the Cold War that soon flared up after 1945 and was abruptly updated in 1950 at the outbreak of the Korean War (the "Korean Shock"). The term stands for a war likely to be fought as a nuclear war, which could destroy a large part of humanity through a nuclear holocaust. In this context, the Third World War also means the Last World War. Let us ardently hope that it never comes to that. The fact is, however, that since 2018 a resurgence in the arms race between nations has been unmistakable.

The world entered the 2020s with 14,465 nuclear warheads. Russia has the most (as of 2020) – 6,850 – followed by the USA with 6,450 nuclear warheads. Incidentally, the third largest nuclear power is not China, as is often assumed but France. The French president commands over three hundred nuclear warheads, China counts 280. In addition, there is a whole series of countries that also possess nuclear weapons: the UK (215), Pakistan (145), India (135), Israel (80) and North Korea (15).[211]

The war triumvirate

In any case, the USA, possibly Russia, possibly China – that is probably the best way to describe the potential involvement of the three superpowers in a Third World War. Bound by NATO, Europe is on the side of the USA. The United Nations is unlikely to play a decisive role. No country from the triumvirate of superpowers – the USA, Russia and China – concedes any significant power to the UN.

As early as 2 March 2015, political scientists Stephan Cohen and John Mearsheimer warned that the USA could provoke a war with Russia. Hardly anyone took notice, the media had more important things to report. That the USA could be planning a military conflict with Russia sounded like a conspiracy theory.[212]

Since 2018, however, the US government has positioned China much more strongly as an enemy. In what sounds like an ultimatum, the US administration demanded in November 2018 that China submit to the demands of the United States, otherwise the country would face an all-out Cold War. The US declared that it had come to Asia to stay. After the Chinese president had shortly before called on the people to prepare for war, this represented a new stage of escalation that further increased the fear of a confrontation between the two superpowers. The danger that the raging trade war could turn into a military war could no longer be dismissed.[213] The US administration of President Joe Biden and Vice President Kamala Harris has so far avoided any war rhetoric. However, the fundamental China-US conflict has not been abated as a result.

Russia's President Vladimir Putin warned as early as in 2019 not to underestimate the looming threat of nuclear war. "If, God forbid, something like this happens, it can lead to the destruction of the whole of civilisation, if not of the whole planet", Putin told the 2019 annual press conference. Unsurprisingly, Putin saw the responsibility for the growing danger on the side of the USA.[214]

USA: First nuclear weapons test in 1945

The development of atomic or nuclear weapons technology began during the Second World War. On 16 July 1945, the USA conducted the first nuclear weapons test. On 6 and 9 August 1945, nuclear bombs were dropped on the Japanese cities of Hiroshima and Nagasaki, claiming hundreds of thousands of victims. The USSR developed nuclear bombs from 1949 onwards. On 30 October 1961, the Soviet Union detonated the Tsar bomb, the most powerful nuclear weapon ever released. During the Cold War, an arms race ensued, at the height of which the two states together possessed around 70,000 nuclear warheads. Towards the end of the Cold War, their joint nuclear arsenal had the explosive power of more than 800,000 Hiroshima bombs.[215]

Cuban Missile Crisis – the world on the brink

On 17 April 1961, communist Cuba, located just outside the gates of the United States of America, was attacked from Guatemala by some 1,300 Cuban exiles in an attempt to depose the Cuban government under Fidel Castro and return the island to Western influence led by the USA. In fact, the aggressors acted with the covert support of the US intelligence agency CIA, as became clear afterwards. But first, the US was brazen enough to deny any involvement in the invasion before the United Nations General Assembly. It was not until days later that US President John F. Kennedy took responsibility for what his administration saw as a failed action; Fidel Castro remained in power. It was a political debacle beyond compare.[216]

Out of the probably justified fear of another US-backed attack, Fidel Castro pursued Cuba's rapprochement with the Soviet Union. A kind of "showdown" in the Cold War occurred in October 1962, when the USSR wanted to station Soviet medium-range ballistic missiles in Cuba, i.e. in the immediate vicinity of the USA. It was a reaction to the previous stationing of US Jupiter medium-range ballistic missiles on a NATO base in Turkey, directly on the border with the Soviet Union.[217] This was too much for John F. Kennedy: the US president threatened to use nuclear weapons. The imminent danger of half the world, or even the entire world, being annihilated by nuclear war never seemed so acute as during the Cuban Missile Crisis. At that time, medium-range nuclear missiles were considered the "non-plus-ultra", because unlike the intercontinental missiles available long before, they could reach enemy territory before the enemy was able to initiate defensive measures or launch a counterattack. But both the leadership of the USSR and the USA shied away from the apocalypse of a nuclear world war. It would have been the third and probably also the last world war of humankind. Finally, it was agreed that the Soviet Union would renounce stationing missiles on Cuba and that, in return, the USA would guarantee not to carry out any further attack on the island. Only after a considerable delay did the USA withdraw its medium-range ballistic missiles from Turkey so as not to look like the loser in the Cuban Missile Crisis.[218]

Both the USA and the USSR drew consequences from this near annihilation of the world. Nuclear power was taken out of the hands of the military and placed directly under the authority of the respective head of government. Since that time, the codes for launching US nuclear weapons have been kept in a briefcase to which only the US president has access; the procedure in Russia has been similar ever since. In 1963, the so-called "hot wire" was established, a direct telex link between the seats of government of both countries, to enable rapid contact in the event of a crisis and to be able to avert an escalation through immediate negotiations. In addition, bilateral negotiations on arms control were initiated. Thus, the Cuban Missile Crisis led to a gradual policy of détente between the two superpowers. For a long time, this phase was characterised by arms-limiting negotiations and agreements such as SALT (Strategic Arms Limitation Talks), ABM (Anti-Ballistic Missile Treaty) or INF (Intermediate Range Nuclear Forces) – mind you, always between the United States of America, on the one hand, and the Soviet Union, on the other.[219]

Exit from disarmament

In autumn 2018, the US government startled the world by announcing that the United States of America would withdraw from the Intermediate-Range Nuclear Forces Treaty, or in short, INF. The bilateral agreement between the USA and the Soviet Union concluded on 8 December 1987, which came into force indefinitely on 1 June 1988, provided for the destruction of all land-based missiles with a range of between 500 and 5500 kilometres. Since this includes both short and medium range nuclear missiles, there was also talk of a "double zero solution". The two states undertook not to build any new missiles with this target radius and to dismantle all existing weapon systems of this type down to the last missile.

However, the USSR had not complied and therefore the USA wanted to terminate the INF Treaty, US President Donald

Trump declared in October 2018.[220] It is possible that Trump's successor in office, Joe Biden, will have the INF Treaty extended. He will presumably focus less on confrontation.

In any case, the United Nations has nothing to do with the disarmament of short- and medium-range nuclear missiles; the INF Treaty is a purely bilateral treaty between the two major nuclear superpowers. Incidentally, this shows that in 1987, as in the entire period since the Second World War, the UN had little or nothing to contribute to one of the most critical issues in global politics – nuclear weapons. Whenever it comes to existential issues for their own countries, the superpowers have always preferred to negotiate directly with each other.

Therefore, Russia had no recourse against the unilateral termination of the INF Treaty by the USA. Only in the face of this situation did the Russian government try to get the backing of the international community. So, it was understandable that Russia introduced a draft resolution to the UN General Assembly in autumn 2018 that was intended to preserve the treaty. Russia's military and state-sponsored media also verbally made every effort to impress with a fire-and-fury statement of their own that the international community was obliged to respond to this situation with a nuclear "doomsday device". [221] The Biden administration may pursue this course in the 2020s.

Missiles against China – and back

No sooner had the US government announced its withdrawal from the INF Treaty than the USA set about moving medium-range ballistic missiles to the Pacific region. Three conclusions can be drawn from this: First, the US was not primarily concerned with terminating the INF Treaty because of the Russian 9M729 cruise missile, the range of which violates the INF treaty. Secondly, the USA considers China to be a more dangerous enemy than Russia and is therefore positioning itself with missiles against China. And thirdly, the US government wants to make itself independent of international treaties in order to be able to act as it sees fit. It is probably only a matter of time before the USA also declares the termination of the START Treaty, which was renewed in January 2021 and which is the only restriction on the two countries' nuclear arsenals. Ultimately, it can be said that the USA is engaged in a new kind of arms race to defend its dominant role literally by any means necessary.

However, those who unilaterally blame the US for the new arms race should also read the "New Defence Strategy Report" issued by China in mid-2019. In it, China attests to the USA's desire to achieve "absolute military superiority" and regards the United States of America as the main adversary in an "increasingly multipolar world", which China by no means regards as peaceful. It regards the USA, which "provokes and intensifies competition between the major countries", as the cause of the nuclear arms race. The report cites the significant increase in arms spending and the increase in nuclear weapons, missile defence, space and internet capabilities as signs and at the same time evidence of this. This would allow the "global strategic stability", in which China sees the world, to be undermined by the US.

However, not only the USA but also the European Union has been increasing its military presence in China's eyes for years, especially in Central and Eastern Europe. This applies both to

NATO and to all considerations of a separate European army. With Russia, China also perceives a visible reinforcement of nuclear and conventional weapons capabilities, according to the 2019 report. China sees itself as a peace-loving power that has not started a war or conflict in 70 years, since the existence of the People's Republic. The USA is branded as the driver behind the ongoing conflicts in the South China Sea, which would have endangered the stability of the entire region with the installation of the THAAD missile defence system. China describes itself as a single entity to which Taiwan, Tibet and "East Turkestan" are indisputable partners.

China describes its nuclear weapons strategy as follows: Maintaining nuclear deterrence, developing space and cyberspace capabilities. China attaches importance to securing its sovereignty and maritime rights as well as its interests abroad but according to the strategy paper does not plan initial operational deployment (first use) of nuclear weapons and – remarkably – neither the threat of such initial operational deployment.

By its own account, China thus classifies itself as a peace-loving country that only needs weapons to defend its legitimate rights against aggressors - first and foremost the USA. The country is obliged to keep pace with the arms race in order to defend itself against unjustified attacks, if necessary. Red lines are identified which, if crossed, will result in China threatening to take countermeasures. That is precisely where the danger lies.

Should the USA actually station land-based medium-range ballistic missiles in the Pacific region as announced, China would be "forced to take countermeasures if the USA makes good on its threat in this part of the world". In this context, intermediate-range ballistic missiles are explicitly classified as offensive weapons. Any country that deploys missiles is said to be directly or indirectly targeting China and Russia.

South Korea, Australia and Japan have been warned not to be fooled by the US. Indeed, the US argues that the stationing of intermediate-range ballistic missiles in the Pacific is primarily for the protection of US allies such as Japan or South Korea.

Incidentally, China does not want to participate in possible negotiations on the dismantling of nuclear weapons because the Chinese potential is negligible compared to the nuclear arsenals of Russia and the USA.[222] However, China is apparently doing everything it can to change this. Admiral Charles Richard, commanding the US nuclear forces, reported at a hearing before the United States Congress in 2021 that a "breathtaking expansion" is underway in China, including a growing arsenal of intercontinental ballistic missiles and new mobile launchers. Also in 2021, satellite images of suspicious construction work in northwest China in the towns of Hami and Yume fuelled suspicions that the country was continuing to stockpile its nuclear arsenal.[223] Analyses of satellite imagery reveal at least 229 silos for intercontinental ballistic missiles, which are the main delivery vehicles for nuclear weapons.[224]

Before 2021, it had been assumed that China had "only" 250 to 350 nuclear missiles. The addition of 229 new missiles would thus be roughly equivalent to a doubling of the nuclear arsenal. This massive expansion is in line with the words of head of state Xi Jinping at celebrations marking the centenary of the founding of the Communist Party in July 2021: China will continue to build a "world-class army" to defend its national interests. He declared:

"The Chinese people will never allow foreign forces to harass, oppress or enslave us".[225]

Destruction of the earth

When it comes to potential destruction of the earth by nuclear weapons, the United Nations traditionally does not have much to say. The Nuclear Non-Proliferation Treaty (NPT) was signed on 1 July 1968 by the United States, the Soviet Union and the United Kingdom, and later by France and China, and entered into force on 5 March 1970. This was in the middle of the Cold War and during the arms race between the two superpowers, the USA and the Soviet Union.

The UN served as a forum for talks on nuclear issues. As early as 1961, Ireland had proposed in the UN General Assembly to ban the proliferation of nuclear technology and in the same year, US President John F. Kennedy also declared before the United Nations: "Every man, woman and child lives under a nuclear sword of Damocles, hanging by the slenderest of threads, capable of being cut at any moment by accident or miscalculation or by madness". The doctrine of nuclear deterrence, i.e. to respond with a nuclear strike and blow up the world in the event of an attack of any kind by the other side, had lost credibility. The balance of terror that had been effective up to then also harboured the danger that nuclear weapons would fall into the hands of other states or even terrorists. In the meantime, more than 190 states have joined the agreement, which is certainly of great symbolic importance but factually insignificant, because most of the signatories do not possess any nuclear weapons at all and the commitment not to acquire any in the future only serves to shed light on what is beyond the planning or reach of these countries. What is crucial is that the five official nuclear powers obtained this status by having detonated a nuclear weapon before 1 January 1967 and then pledged "to conduct negotiations in good faith on a treaty for general and complete disarmament under strict and effective international control".

This is the only binding commitment to complete disarmament by the nuclear powers in the multilateral treaty. It is remarkable, however, that four states have not signed the Nuclear Non-Proliferation Treaty: India, Israel, Pakistan and South Sudan, although at least two of them – Israel and Pakistan – undoubtedly have nuclear weapons. North Korea withdrew from the treaty in January 2003 and has likely entered the 2020s with warhead-sized nuclear weapons that fit ballistic missiles.[226] Thus, one can summarise: The Nuclear Non-Proliferation Treaty was a good idea while it lasted and it did not harm the world but it is questionable whether it is useful for the superpowers to negotiate directly in the absence of a number of nuclear states.

Another obstacle to the implementation of the treaty was that it granted each participating state the "inalienable right" to a civilian nuclear programme. Far beyond this, all signatories to the treaty committed themselves to "facilitate the widest possible exchange of equipment, materials and scientific and technological information for the peaceful use of nuclear energy". In other words: Each signatory to the treaty may develop and use as much nuclear energy as it wants, as long as this falls under civilian use. This is precisely the crux: whoever wants to develop nuclear weapons will claim as long as possible that this development is only for civilian purposes. It goes even further: the signatories have pledged to support each other in the use of nuclear energy – again, exclusively for peaceful purposes, of course. This can work well as long as everyone participates voluntarily and, above all, willingly. But at the same time, it opens the floodgates to all those who wish to exploit it.

After all, the treaty provided for a certain amount of control among all participating states as to whether they were abiding by the agreement. For this purpose, a new authority, the International Atomic Energy Agency (IAEA), was founded. Just as the UN was not involved in the conclusion of the nuclear treaty, the new nuclear authority was not subordinated to it. To this day, the IAEA is not a specialised agency of the United Nations but an autonomous scientific and technical organisation, which is nevertheless affiliated with the UN by separate agreement. Under this treaty, the nuclear authority reports to the UN, and regularly to the General Assembly and beyond that to the UN Security Council, if it identifies a threat to international security.[227] In other words, it does not report to the UN and the UN has no authority to issue directives but it is closely affiliated to five nuclear-weapon nations through the Security Council. This is tantamount to the United Nations being in an extremely weak position on one of the key issues facing humanity – namely, potential annihilation through nuclear power – while the IAEA itself is certainly endowed with a certain amount of power. Thus, the Statute stipulates that the Agency shall "accelerate and enlarge the contribution of atomic energy to peace, health and prosperity throughout the world". In doing so, it should promote the use of radioactive substances and international cooperation, as well as prevent the military use of this technology through surveillance measures. For this, it was awarded the Nobel Peace Prize in 2005 together with its then Secretary General Mohammed al-Baradei.

Just how little the USA thought of the International Atomic Energy Agency became clear a year earlier when it became publicly known that they had illegally wiretapped the Nobel Peace Prize laureate in order to force him out of office with incriminating material. There was a simple reason for this: Mohammed al-Baradei had previously convicted the then US President George W. Bush of a downright lie when he ordered the attack on Iraq in March 2003 on the grounds that this country possessed nuclear weapons of mass destruction. Subsequent IAEA investigations clearly demonstrated that this assessment was wrong, and it became equally clear that the US government was aware of this.[228]

Abuse of the UN

What was notable in the 2013 Iraq war was the abuse of the United Nations by the US. Iraq is alleged to have violated UN resolutions against it by both developing and possessing weapons of mass destruction. This, as it turned out later, was downright wrong. Meanwhile: When the United States under Bush attacked Iraq in March 2003, it was unable to invoke either self-defence or a United Nations Security Council resolution. Therefore, Bush's war was legally a crime, namely aggression. This – along with genocide, war crimes and crimes against humanity – is one of the core offences in international criminal law. The accusation that Iraq harboured nuclear weapons thus had to be used as a pretext for waging a war of aggression in defiance of the UN, which can probably be classified as revenge against the attacks of 11

September 2001. The terrorist organisation Al-Qaeda was suspected to have been behind the attacks and a link to the Iraqi dictator Saddam Hussein was established. No sensible person will bemoan the fall of this dictator, nor the dismantling of the terrorist group. But that does not change anything about the contemptuous actions of the USA towards the UN.

Incidentally, the United States, together with the United Kingdom, interpreted UN Resolution 1441 as an attack mandate – against the express opposition of the other members in the Security Council. The resolution, adopted on 8 November 2002, called on Iraq to accept unconditionally the previous Security Council resolutions and to grant the International Atomic Energy Agency free and unrestricted access to arms producing facilities. In addition, it was to divest itself of all biological and biochemical weapons. Since Iraq did not initially comply with these demands, the USA regarded its attack on the country as justified, especially since the political scenario had been portrayed that Iraq was on the verge of attacking the USA. Incidentally, the United Nations has never condemned this action – every attempt to do so failed due to the veto power of the USA in the Security Council.

Nevertheless, it remains unforgotten how the then IAEA Secretary-General Mohammed al-Barāda systematically deconstructed the allegedly so unmistakable evidence of a resumed atomic bomb programme of Iraq in the UN Security Council thus disgracing the Bush administration in the eyes of the international community. The Intelligence Committee of the US Senate also subsequently came to the clear conclusion that the reasons for the attack were false and purely fabricated.

But even more devastating than the reasons were the consequences: During the Iraq war, the terrorist group "Islamic State" (IS) gained unprecedented momentum. The US aggression not only changed the entire region but also has a direct impact on Europe to this day. The foundations were laid for the Syrian conflict, which not only resulted in the deaths of thousands of people but also brought millions of refugees to Europe, which in turn served to boost the growth of right-wing populism in almost all European countries.[229]

The impotence of international organisations

The Iraq war once again exemplified the paralysis of international organisations such as the United Nations or the International Atomic Energy Agency when it comes to asserting themselves vis-à-vis the interests of the superpowers. However, this in no way prevents the international organisations from addressing the respective issue in ever new resolutions, protocols and conferences.

The IAEA therefore saw itself restricted in that, although it could certainly conduct on-site inspections in nuclear facilities, it had to notify them and therefore gave the state under inspection the opportunity to remove any nuclear weapons out of the inspectors' sights. Promptly, the nuclear authority adopted an Additional Protocol to the Nuclear Non-Proliferation Treaty, which enabled inspectors to conduct unannounced inspections at any facility. To monitor compliance with the treaty, review conferences have been held every five years since 1995, for example in New York from 27 April to 22 May 2015. At the 1995 conference, the treaty, which was initially only designed for 25 years, was extended for an indefinite period but its effectiveness was not reinforced. Thus, although 13 steps towards complete nuclear disarmament were agreed at the 2000 conference, the very next conference in 2005 remained inconclusive due to the blockade by the USA. As we entered the 2020s, more nuclear explosive power was distributed around the world than ever before.

Just as the Security Council at the United Nations had firmly established the supremacy of a few superpowers from the outset, the Nuclear Non-Proliferation Treaty established an imbalance: while the official nuclear powers may maintain their arsenals, all other states are prohibited from pursuing nuclear rearmament. At the same time, there is no sign of disarmament by the official superpowers.

The allegation that the superpowers are thus merely masking their own power interests through international organisations such as the UN or the IAEA stands to reason. This is all the more true since the nuclear powers specified in the Nuclear Non-Proliferation Treaty are at the same time the permanent members of the UN Security Council, where they have the right of veto and can block attempts under international law to persuade them to disarm. Moreover, one must ask whether the nuclear powers, which have already waged wars of aggression across the board, have the moral justification to impose regulations on other states about their armament.

The Nuclear Non-Proliferation Treaty is downright ineffective. Neither are the superpowers disarming nor are other states being prevented from equipping themselves with nuclear weapons. India and Pakistan have long since confirmed that they have nuclear weapons, and Israel has long been suspected of having them. North Korea experimented with several nuclear bombs until September 2017, and most recently, even a hydrogen bomb, before the country announced the cessation of testing on 21 April 2018.

South Africa is considered a "prime example" of how UN resolutions are undermined by states. The country had pursued a nuclear weapons programme since 1969 but voluntarily ended it in the early 1990s. In the meantime, South Africa has joined the Nuclear Non-Proliferation Treaty but apparently still has the capacity to re-engage in a nuclear weapons programme after withdrawing from the treaty.[230]

Since 2018, Iran has been at the centre of the global nuclear debate. In May 2018, US President Trump declared the withdrawal from the agreement to prevent an Iranian nuclear bomb, which had been in force until then, and put sanctions against the country into effect. Shortly afterwards, the country's supreme leader, Ayatollah Ali Khamenei, announced his plan to resume unlimited uranium enrichment, i.e. to create the conditions for military nuclear use.

The anti-nuclear agreement with Iran was signed in 2015 not only by the USA but also by the United Kingdom, France, Germany, China and Russia. These countries also wanted to adhere to the agreement in 2019. But the US government's pressure on these countries to go along with the US sanctions already had an effect in 2018, and European companies visibly withdrew from doing business with Iran. The fear of acting against the explicit will of the USA was apparently too great.[231] The question of the attitude of the United Nations on this issue did not even arise because it was irrelevant.

China no longer rules out FIRST nuclear strike

In early autumn 2021, China's former ambassador to the United Nations, Sha Zukang, reportedly stated the almost unthinkable: China must abandon its "no-first-use" policy on the use of nuclear bombs. Until then, this policy stipulated that China must always be ready to respond to an attack by another nuclear power but must never be the first to launch a nuclear attack itself. China has been considered a nuclear power since 1964 and introduced the "no-first-use" policy four years later. After the USA had deliberately dropped the world's first nuclear bombs against the civilian population of Japan on 6 and 9 August 1945, China at least no longer wanted to rule out such a step, a third nuclear bomb, in 2021. The US has committed not to use nuclear weapons against most other countries but has explicitly excluded China, Russia and North Korea from this commitment.

China's paradigm shift was preceded by the announcement of a US military alliance with Australia, called AUKUS, to equip the Australian continent with nuclear-powered submarines for the first time. The nuclear advance of the USA in 2021 was to be seen as a direct counterbalance to China's rearmament in the Pacific. This was compounded in 2021 by another alliance between the US, India, Japan and Australia, called Quad, in which US President Joe Biden claimed leadership and focused on security issues in the face of the rising threat from China.[232] All these developments obviously led to China no longer ruling out a first strike since 2021.

However, even with its latest nuclear rearmament programmes, China is still far behind the USA and Russia. China entered 2022 with a maximum of 1,000 nuclear warheads, while the US and Russia each have around 4,000 nuclear warheads.[233]

Pathways to Peace

The speed at which peace is rapidly eluding us in today's world is of great concern to any reasonable and perceptive person. People who consider themselves educated and civilised are reverting to the time when personal egoism and false pride led people to go for each other's throats, and on a communal basis led tribes and dynasties to indulge in barbaric acts.

Today we must conclude that wars are not a thing of the past; on the contrary, they are more acute than ever before. We have to see that when governments challenge other governments to achieve their political and economic goals, it is always the poor and peace-loving citizens of those countries who suffer during the ensuing tension. They are caught between the millstones of hunger, poverty and savagery. Where is the fault of those children who do not even understand these arguments about political and economic superiority?

World War III can be averted

The seemingly inevitable clash of China and the USA, the resurgence of Russia, the pact of the two communist states to form a new "Sino-Soviet bloc", the reorientation of NATO, new weaponry and the open threat of an increasing number of internet warriors – none of these are good harbingers for our future. Added to this are ever-stronger terrorist organisations, new forms of warfare and new theatres of war. Therefore, it seems almost inevitable that our civilisation is heading for a Third World War. But in fact, such a catastrophe can be averted.

Since 1945, the United Nations has been a supranational organisation in which all states have had a voice. The UN still defends a marvellous vision: it is the idea that beyond all national interests there is a global, quasi overriding interest of all states, all citizens and organisations that can be defined and implemented with the help of all participants. The experiences of the past decades have blatantly exposed the weaknesses of the UN, as illustrated in many passages in this book. This is attributable to several factors.

Firstly, the veto power of the superpowers turns out to be an inherent flaw in the structure of the UN. It is as if, in an independent court, the prosecutor or the defendant could simply dispute the verdict and thus render it ineffective – what authority would such a court have?

Secondly, the United Nations has unfortunately developed into a kind of monster bureaucracy that takes care of really everything but can hardly achieve anything. All attempts to reduce or minimise this bureaucracy through reforms have failed so far.

Thirdly, nationalist traits are making their way into political power almost everywhere in the world. The rise of nationalism would make a supranational organisation like the UN seem more important than ever but precisely this nationalism explains why states do not want to be told what to do by a supranational institution like the UN. The G3 powers China, Russia and the United States regard the UN primarily as an instrument to advance their interests. As soon as the United Nations does not seem useful to them, they simply ignore it.

Happy place and non-place Utopia

This is largely due to the fact that the UN's utopias for improving the world have become extremely far removed from the political realities in the individual states and from people's everyday lives. The United Nations publicly dreams of a world where all people can live in peace and freedom with the best health care. These events are reminiscent of the philosophical dialogue "De optimo statu rei publicae deque nova insula Utopia" ("A little, true book, not less beneficial than enjoyable, about how things should be in a state and about the new island Utopia") written in Latin in 1516 by the English statesman Thomas Morus, in which, probably following Plato's dialogue "Timaeus", he describes a fictitious island empire with an "ideal" society, which is considered the birth of social utopia. The Greek word "utopia" can be translated as "happy place" or as "dystopia," depending on whether one counts oneself among the pessimists or the optimists. Similarly, in view of the tripartite struggle between China, Russia and the United States, the assessment of the United Nations is probably more a matter of perception than reality.

But a think tank like the Diplomatic Council cannot and will not cede responsibility for peace processes solely to the international institutions, nor to the most powerful state on earth. There are key elements to mitigating conflict that, if considered, always steer the way towards peace. These are:

1. Ensure legitimacy both of all participants and of the peace process.

2. Take diplomatic measures to enter or remain in dialogue.
3. Work towards reconciliation, conciliation and mediation.
4. Flexibility and willingness to compromise for the sake of peace.
5. Principle of proportionality in all measures.
6. Seek, emphasise and strengthen commonalities.
7. Completely avoid aggression of any kind.
8. Negotiations through dialogue and collaboration.
9. Show responsibility and passion for the solution.
10. All sensationalism is detrimental to success.

The United Nations would be well-advised to do the same. But carrots and sticks are no option for the UN. The point is rather to boost the efficiency of the United Nations. The pessimists may lament the ineffectiveness and predict the demise of the United Nations.

The optimists will not let the UN's impotence prevent them from believing in progress towards a better humanity. The authors of this book consider themselves among the optimists based on the realisation that while the United Nations is far from perfect, as demonstrated in countless instances throughout this book, it is the best we have. Let us continue to improve the UN rather than abolish it – and let us not give up hope that it can prevent the Third World War.

About the authors

Andreas Dripke

Andreas Dripke has been an author, analyst, editor-in-chief and journalist for over 30 years. He has written more than 20 non-fiction books, authored dozens of analytical and market reports and published well over 100 articles. His works are characterised by the fact that they describe key topics in a carefully researched and extremely gripping and comprehensible manner.

At the Diplomatic Council, a global think tank with consultative status at the United Nations (UN), and publisher of this book, he has participated in many non-public UN conferences as CEO to the United Nations. The diverse insights, knowledge and contacts gained at the highest level have been integrated into all his publications.

Today, in his capacity as Executive Chairman of the Diplomatic Council, Andreas Dripke deals with current issues of geopolitical and social significance.

Hang Nguyen

Hang Nguyen came to Germany as a child seeking refuge from the Vietnam War. She has experienced first-hand the misery of a war that only broke out because the superpowers sought war and the United Nations could not find a way to peace. Today she says about her escape: "I only survived because complete strangers took care of me".

From this experience, she has developed an ardent desire to help other people, as she was once helped. As Secretary General of the Diplomatic Council, she is the face and the heart of the organisation that published this work.

She would like nothing better than a perfectly functioning UN that brings peace to humanity everywhere. But in her work at the Diplomatic Council, she has had to learn that the United Nations still has a long road ahead. This book is her reminder to the world's largest supranational organisation to prevent World War III at all costs.

Jamal Qaiser

Jamal Qaiser made his way from teenage market trader to investor and CEO of his private equity firm. In 2010 he started the Advance Management Diploma (Post-Graduation) at the Globe Business College in Munich. In 2013, he began studying "Owner/President Management" at the renowned Harvard Business School, which he successfully completed in 2016. During that time, he completed the Transition to Leadership Programme at the University of Oxford Said Business School in 2014.

Far beyond his successful academic and business endeavours, Jamal Qaiser finds inspiration in contributing to world peace. He advises governments, NGOs, humanist organisations, international corporations and, last but not least, the United Nations in the Diplomatic Council (DC) as DC Commissioner for UN Affairs.

This publication, "When China and Russia join forces", is his sixth book on global political developments. His books have won international awards, including the prestigious getAbstract Book Award from a selection of over 10,000 non-fiction books.

In a contribution from UN circles, he was once characterised as follows: "Jamal Qaiser is an extremely bright mind with a clear sense of mission for justice and humanity. He clearly enjoys his role as an active consultant for people and organisations to foster positive development. Determination coupled with the right goals of international understanding are essential to his nature".

Books published by DC (English)

My nuclear button is bigger — America vs. North Korea. Jamal Qaiser, 184 pages, paperback, ISBN 978-3-947818-01-3

How to avoid the World War III – A plea for peace, Hang Nguyen, Jamal Qaiser, 268 pages, paperback, ISBN 978-3-947818-67-9

The Western Fiasco: Failure in Afghanistan, Syria and Ukraine, Hang Nguyen, Jamal Qaiser, 148 pages, paperback, ISBN 978-3-947818-97-6

Simmering Kashmir, Jamal Qaiser, Sadaf Taimur, 110 pages, paperback, ISBN 978-3-947818-11-2

Afghanistan - The Battered Land, Jamal Qaiser, Sadaf Taimur, 112 pages, paperback, ISBN 978-3-98674-003-0

About the Diplomatic Council

This work is published by the Diplomatic Council (DC): DC Publishing.

The Diplomatic Council combines a global think tank, a worldwide business network and a charity foundation into a unique organisation with consultative status at the United Nations.

Our members passionately believe that economic diplomacy is a fundamental basis for international understanding and peaceful relations between nations. Based on this insight, the Diplomatic Council translates the goal of global international understanding into an economic mandate. To this end, the methodology of a global economic network is connected to the diplomatic level of communication between the nations of the world.Against this background, the Diplomatic Council is staffed by personalities the diplomatic, business and social spheres who are selected with a sound sense of judgement and who are characterised by a high degree of acceptance, a high degree of competence and a value system that is aligned with the key principles of the Diplomatic Council. Companies for which corporate social responsibility is much more than a buzzword are also welcome.

For further Information, see: www.diplomatic-council.org/application

References and Notes

[1] https://www.dhm.de/lemo/kapitel/erster-weltkrieg/kriegsverlauf/tod-und-verwundung.html

[2] https://www.welt.de/geschichte/zweiter-weltkrieg/article140814551/Pro-Stunde-starben-100-deutsche-Soldaten.html

[3] Zehnter Band der vom Militärgeschichtlichen Forschungsamt der Bundeswehr herausgegebenen Reihe „Das deutsche Reich und der Zweite Weltkrieg 2008"

[4] Ernst Sauer: Grundlehre des Völkerrechts, 2. Auflage, Verlag Balduin Pick, Köln, 1948

[5] Thomas J. Knock: *To End All Wars: Woodrow Wilson and the Quest for a New World Order*. Princeton University Press, 1995, ISBN 0-691-00150-2

[6] https://internationalepolitik.de/de/die-kriege-des-jahres-2016

[7] https://hiik.de

[8] https://hiik.de/wp-content/uploads/2021/05/ConflictBarometer_2020_2.pdf

[9] https://www.news.de/panorama/855219366/wie-viele-menschen-sterben-taeglich-in-deutschland-todesursachen-herzinfarkt-krieg-suizid/1/

[10] https://www.globalresearch.ca/u-s-regime-has-killed-20-30-million-people-since-world-war-ii/5633111

[11] https://www.handelsblatt.com/dpa/konjunktur/wirtschaft-handel-und-finanzen-russischer-aussenminister-lawrow-wirft-westen-nukleare-panikmache-vor/28126580.html

[12] https://www.tagesanzeiger.ch/warum-die-usa-betont-kuehl-auf-putins-nukleare-drohung-reagieren-415969871888

[13] https://www.welt.de/politik/ausland/article208063073/Stimmungsbild-USA-oder-China-Die-Deutschen-sind-tief-gespalten.html

[14] https://www.zeit.de/politik/ausland/2021-07/usa-angela-merkel-joe-biden-abschiedsbesuch-washington-nord-stream-2-corona

[15] https://www.deutschlandfunk.de/100-jahre-kommunistische-partei-chinas-eine-staatspartei-100.html

[16] https://ome-lexikon.uni-oldenburg.de/laender/russische-foederation

[17] https://www.nzz.ch/international/mao-deng-und-xi-100-jahre-kommunistische-partei-chinas-ld.1630335

[18] https://www.britannica.com/biography/Deng-Xiaoping

[19] https://www.spiegel.de/ausland/china-so-feiert-das-land-den-100-jahrestag-der-kommunistischen-partei-a-36ca1892-c846-4145-9c89-26777393a216

[20] https://www.dw.com/de/wladimir-putin-ermöglicht-sich-weitere-amtszeiten/a-57104503

[21] https://www.deutschlandfunk.de/us-strategie-gegen-china-biden-sucht-verbuendete-aber-er.694.de.html

[22] https://www.focus.de/politik/deutschland/was-spricht-dagegen-schroeder-erklaert-in-bizarrem-interview-warum-deutschland-sich-mit-china-verbuenden-muss_id_9929681.html
[23] https://www.bild.de/regional/bremen/bremen-aktuell/neue-seidenstrasse-erster-gueterzug-aus-china-rollt-an-77076222.bild.html
[24] https://www.spiegel.de/ausland/joe-bidens-erste-pressekonferenz-erst-euphorisch-dann-vage-dann-genervt-a-89c04f4b-7449-44af-b7eb-24d386295362
[25] https://www.swp-berlin.org/publikation/der-amerikanisch-chinesische-weltkonflikt
[26] https://www.swr.de/swr2/wissen/archivradio/aexavarticle-swr-42278.html
[27] https://www.zeit.de/politik/ausland/2018-11/vereinte-nationen-carla-del-ponte-reform-uno-buerokratie
[28] https://www.zdnet.de/88356411/artikel-13-und-uploadfilter-un-sonderberichterstatter-sieht-meinungsfreiheit-in-gefahr/
[29] https://www.tagesspiegel.de/politik/soziale-menschenrechte-un-sozialrat-wirft-deutschland-defizite-vor/23782562.html
[30] https://www.economist.com/china/2021/03/31/china-is-betting-that-the-west-is-in-irreversible-decline
[31] https://www.un.org/es/node/44721
[32] https://www.unaa.org.au/wp-content/uploads/2015/07/UNAA_UNDAY_factsheet_v1.pdf
[33] https://www.diplomatic-council.org/de/node/848
[34] 75 Jahre UNO – Macht und Ohnmacht der Vereinten Nationen, Andreas Dripke, Hang Nguyen, DC Publishing, ISBN 978-3-947818-07-5
[35] https://zeitschrift-vereinte-nationen.de/suche/zvn/artikel/die-volksrepublik-china-und-die-vereinten-nationen/
[36] https://www.bpb.de/politik/hintergrund-aktuell/208696/un-charta
[37] https://www.spiegel.de/politik/ausland/corona-krise-usa-stoppen-uno-resolution-zur-pandemie-a-675b25c8-4912-487f-8c14-3f5ab89bf686
[38] https://www.deutschlandfunk.de/teilung-koreas-1945-grundstein-eines-konflikts-der-bis.724.de.html?dram:article_id=483761
[39] https://www1.wdr.de/stichtag/stichtag-sowjetunion-erste-atombombe-100.html
[40] https://www.manager-magazin.de/politik/weltwirtschaft/deutschland-tritt-aiib-bei-china-spaltet-westen-mit-bank-a-1024354.html
[41] https://www.welt.de/geschichte/zweiter-weltkrieg/gallery114766339/General-Douglas-MacArthur-1880-1964-Stationen.html
[42] https://www.fordlibrarymuseum.gov/library/document/0337/24468967.pdf
[43] Matray, Dictionary 1991, pg. 496, Matray, James L. (publisher): Historical Dictionary of the Korean War, Greenwood Publishing Group Inc, New York, Westport, London. 1991, Day, Myong-Sig: US foreign policy towards 1942 – 1955 – with special reference to the division of Korea, the Korean War and the role of the UN, dissertation, Heinrich Heine University Düsseldorf 1995
[44] Loth, Wilfried: Die Teilung der Welt – Geschichte des Kalten Krieges 1941 – 1955, S. 380, Deutscher Taschenbuch Verlag GmbH & Co. KG, München 2000
[45] https://www.un.org/en/sc/repertoire/otherdocs/GAres377A(v).pdf
[46] https://www.spiegel.de/spiegel/print/d-29193879.html
[47] https://digitallibrary.un.org/record/669433

[48] https://www.un.org/disarmament/wp-content/uploads/2017/02/A-2361-Add2.pdf
[49] Artikel in der New York Times 1966 von Drew Middleton: "U Thant Denounces Vietnam War; Proposes Three Steps to Peace"

[50] https://www.nybooks.com/articles/1966/11/17/u-thant-and-vietnam-the-untold-story/
[51] Zhai Qiang: China and the Geneva Conference of 1954. In: The China Quarterly. No. 129. Cambridge University Press, March 1992
[52] https://www.tagesschau.de/ausland/usa-exportverbot-impfstoff-101.html
[53] https://www.merkur.de/politik/impfdiplomatie-china-export-corona-impfstoff-welt-bedarf-sinopharm-ungarn-serbien-afrika-90214624.html
[54] https://www.nzz.ch/international/uno-generalversammlung-china-schreibt-die-werte-der-uno-um-ld.1577845
[55] https://www.ipinst.org/wp-content/uploads/2016/09/ICM-Final-Report-rev.pdf
[56] https://www.stern.de/politik/ausland/frueherer-us-sicherheitsberater-bolton-warnt-vor-atomwaffen-im-besitz-der-taliban-30665932.html
[57] https://www.nzz.ch/international/die-usa-treten-aus-dem-uno-menschenrechts-rat-aus-ld.1396356?reduced=true
[58] https://www.msn.com/de-de/nachrichten/politics/sind-ein-europischer-staat-georgien-bewirbt-sich-um-eumitgliedschaft/ar-AAUyTle?ocid=sapphireappshare
[59] https://www.destatis.de/Europa/DE/Staat/Beitrittskandidaten/_inhalt.html
[60] https://www.deutschlandfunk.de/militaerisches-buendnis-die-nato-und-die-causa-tuerkei-100.html
[61] https://www.handelsblatt.com/politik/international/ukraine-krieg-wie-finnland-und-schweden-einen-nato-beitritt-diskutieren/28118414.html
[62] https://www.rnd.de/politik/moeglicher-nato-beitritt-von-finnland-und-schweden-russland-fordert-sicherheitsgarantien-6QQBDPPQFVGR7C75BQJSMOSFQE.html
[63] https://www.t-online.de/nachrichten/ausland/internationale-politik/id_85133976/weltwirtschaftsforum-in-davos-angela-merkel-plaediert-fuer-neue-weltordnung.html
[64] https://www.spiegel.de/wirtschaft/unternehmen/russland-wladimir-putins-wirtschaftsbilanz-nach-18-jahren-a-1198313.html
[65] https://www.merkur.de/politik/china-feiert-mit-militaerparade-superlative-zr-13055811.html
[66] https://www.spiegel.de/ausland/china-draengt-offenbar-us-zerstoerer-im-suedchinesischen-meer-ab-a-cfade81e-42cb-4cc8-9dbc-0a9f846a1a64
[67] https://www.deutschlandfunk.de/schiedsgericht-in-den-haag-china-hat-keine.2852.de.html
[68] https://www.spiegel.de/ausland/folge-von-cyberangriff-us-praesident-joe-biden-warnt-vor-echtem-krieg-a-66f2acff-7baa-4af5-85b4-0a4c8d30de6b
[69] https://www.faz.net/aktuell/politik/russland-nachrichtenagentur-feiert-irrtuemlich-sieg-ueber-ukraine-17840071.html
[70] Birgitte Refslund Sørensen/Marc Vincent: *Caught Between Borders: Response Strategies of the Internally Displaced*, Pluto Press 2001, ISBN 0-7453-1818-5.

[71] Nikola Cvetkovski: *The Georgian-South-Ossetian Conflict;* Danish Association for Research on the Caucasus 2009, Chapter 4.4 „Combatants and the Natur of Warfare."

[72] Pilar Bonet: *Guerra en el Cáucaso Rusia interviene en el Cáucaso para quedarse y controlar su espacio vital.* In: El País, 17. August 2008

[73] https://www.tagesschau.de/ausland/ukraine114.html

[74] https://www.businessinsider.de/politik/welt/so-brutal-agiert-putins-wagner-group/

https://web.archive.org/web/20100422121915/http:/ec.europa.eu/external_relations/ukraine/index_en.htm

Birgitte Refslund Sørensen/Marc Vincent: *Caught Between Borders: Response Strategies of the Internally Displaced*, Pluto Press 2001, S. 234–235. ISBN 0-7453-1818-5.

[75] https://www.nzz.ch/international/ukraine-chronologie-der-maidan-revolution-ld.1290571

[76] https://www.zeit.de/politik/ausland/2014-09/russland-soldaten-ukraine-staatsfernsehen

[77] https://www.cbc.ca/news/world/pro-russian-rebels-officially-labelled-terrorists-by-ukraine-government-1.2933845

[78] https://www.ohchr.org/documents/countries/ua/hrmmureport15june2014.pdf

[79] https://www.ohchr.org/EN/NewsEvents/Pages/DisplayNews.aspx

[80] https://www.faz.net/aktuell/politik/ausland/europa/ukrainekonflikt-von-wegen-waffenruhe-13511725.html

[81] https://www.tagesanzeiger.ch/ausland/europa/die-gewalt-kann-jederzeit-gestoppt-werden/story/13734340

[82] https://www.nzz.ch/meinung/debatte/der-krim-konflikt-und-das-voelkerrecht-1.18265005

[83] https://www.zeit.de/politik/ausland/2015-03/putin-krim-annexion

[84] https://www.un.org/en/ga/search/view_doc.asp?symbol=A/RES/68/262

[85] https://www.dw.com/de/marine-experte-krim-ist-russlands-sprungbrett-ins-mittelmeer/a-17463353

[86] https://ru.wikisource.org/wiki/Федеральный_конституционный_закон_от_21.03.2014_№_6-ФКЗ

[87] https://www.stern.de/politik/ausland/ukraine--was-hinter-der-anerkennung-der--volksrepubliken--steckte-31650072.html

[88] https://www.nytimes.com/2012/11/16/opinion/the-worlds-next-genocide.html

[89] https://www.reuters.com/article/us-syria-ceasefire/text-of-annans-six-point-peace-plan-for-syria-idUSBRE8330HJ20120404

[90] https://www.securitycouncilreport.org/atf/cf/%7B65BFCF9B-6D27-4E9C-8CD3-CF6E4FF96FF9%7D/Syria%20SRES%202043.pdf

[91] https://www.nytimes.com/2013/09/17/world/europe/syria-united-nations.html

[92] https://www.dailyrecord.co.uk/news/uk-world-news/its-time-use-force-syria-2210357

[93] https://www.reuters.com/article/us-syria-crisis-chemicalweapons-exclusiv/exclusive-tests-link-syrian-government-stockpile-to-largest-sarin-attack-sources-idUSKBN1FJ0MG

[94] https://www.defense.gov/Explore/News/Article/Article/603271/
[95]https://web.archive.org/web/20170201172657/https:/www.defensie.nl/english/topics/iraq/contents/dutch-military-contribution
[96] https://www.kas.de/de/laenderberichte/detail/-/content/tunesien-im-arabischen-fruehling
[97] https://www.amica-ev.org/amica-in-libyen/10-jahre-revolution/
[98] https://www.vorwaerts.de/artikel/arabischer-fruehling-aegypten-gescheiterte-revolution
[99] https://www.spiegel.de/politik/ausland/wladimir-putin-wirft-petro-poroschenko-provokation-in-kertsch-vor-a-1244752.html
[100] https://www.zdf.de/nachrichten/politik/ukraine-krieg-russland-proteste-100.html
[101] https://www.welt.de/politik/ausland/video237112641/Angriff-auf-Ukraine-Putin-ordnet-besondere-Militaeroperation-an.html
[102] https://www.rnd.de/politik/ukraine-wolodymyr-selenskyis-mut-verbluefft-freund-und-feind-DGR2T4BXS5AW3EJP2W5ADASRJY.html
[103] https://www.spiegel.de/ausland/ukraine-russland-krieg-reaktionen-auf-deutsche-waffen-lieferungen-an-die-ukraine-a-ea36e6c0-0701-4e9d-93dd-2426f872764a
[104] https://www.spiegel.de/politik/deutschland-genehmigt-panzerfaust-lieferungen-an-die-ukraine-a-9e051204-4c43-4c42-a0e6-e00d484c716f
[105] https://www.spiegel.de/ausland/russland-ukraine-news-am-samstag-wolodymyr-selenskyj-erwartet-russischen-sturm-auf-kiew-noch-diese-nacht-a-d5b90774-e2c4-4048-9fe7-961d47e5ed3f
[106] https://www.sueddeutsche.de/politik/konflikte-ukraine-stimmt-verhandlungen-mit-russland-zu-dpa.urn-newsml-dpa-com-20090101-220227-99-310200
[107] https://www.n-tv.de/politik/Botschafter-Melnyk-lobt-deutsche-Waffenlieferungen-article23158667.html
[108] https://www.sueddeutsche.de/politik/konflikte-scholz-erklaert-sich-nach-kurswechsel-in-der-ukraine-krise-dpa.urn-newsml-dpa-com-20090101-220226-99-300593
[109] https://www.welt.de/politik/ausland/article237140631/Russland-Deutschlands-Unterwerfung-Geschichte-eines-historischen-Versagens.html
[110] https://www.mdr.de/geschichte/zeitgeschichte-gegenwart/freundschaft-schroeder-putin-russland-ukraine-gazprom-nordstream-lobbyismus-100.html
[111] https://www.bmwi.de/Redaktion/DE/Artikel/Aussenwirtschaft/laendervermerk-china.html
[112] https://www.focus.de/finanzen/boerse/insider-berichten-in-china-brennt-die-huette-koennte-das-geschaeft-in-fernost-diess-den-job-kosten_id_24427697.html
[113] https://www.spiegel.de/ausland/russland-krieg-in-der-ukraine-westliche-staaten-schliessen-russische-banken-aus-swift-aus-a-a8ba2a6f-fc59-4d6c-9962-c39967e4c1ef
[114] https://de.wikipedia.org/wiki/SWIFT
[115] https://ec.europa.eu/commission/presscorner/detail/de/statement_22_1422
[116] https://www.tagesschau.de/wirtschaft/weltwirtschaft/rubel-absturz-sanktionen-krieg-ukraine-101.html

[117] https://www.focus.de/politik/ausland/ukraine-krieg-mehrere-russische-medien-nicht-erreichbar-weil-anonymous-sie-gehackt-hat_id_60717133.html
[118] https://www.dailymail.co.uk/news/article-10549849/Hacking-collective-Anonymous-declares-cyber-war-against-Vladimir-Putins-government.html
[119] https://www.spiegel.de/ausland/ukraine-maulkorb-fuer-russlands-kriegsgegner-a-1173a5af-6aea-4739-b4cc-6fe2a37eebd4
[120] https://www.zdf.de/nachrichten/politik/ukraine-krieg-russland-proteste-100.html
[121] https://www.zeit.de/politik/ausland/2022-02/wladimir-putin-versetzt-atomstreitkraefte-in-alarmbereitschaft
[122] https://www.handelsblatt.com/dpa/konjunktur/wirtschaft-handel-und-finanzen-russischer-aussenminister-lawrow-wirft-westen-nukleare-panikmache-vor/28126580.html
[123] https://www.tagesspiegel.de/politik/laut-macron-steht-das-schlimmste-noch-bevor-putin-droht-der-ukraine-mit-neuen-forderungen/28126776.html
[124] https://www.rnd.de/politik/krieg-in-der-ukraine-elon-musk-aktiviert-starlink-satelliten-fuer-internet-in-der-ukraine-LRTUT55MZ2USOOOPGWV7TQSKWQ.html
[125] https://www.zeit.de/politik/ausland/2022-02/ukrainischer-praesident-selenskyj-ruft-kriegszustand-aus
[126] https://www.nw.de/nachrichten/nachrichten/23202220_Bewegende-Videobotschaften-Was-sagt-Selenskyj.html
[127] https://www.tagesschau.de/ausland/asien/china-aussenpolitik-107.html
[128] https://www.spiegel.de/ausland/richard-nixon-und-china-war-der-besuch-des-us-praesidenten-vor-50-jahren-ein-fehler-a-0aa4c5a3-5b3a-43cc-b098-5f6e2cb71a06
[129] https://www.tagesspiegel.de/politik/hilfe-aus-peking-fuer-putin-der-russische-praesident-ist-in-die-falle-getappt/28089950.html
[130] https://www.tagesschau.de/ausland/europa/fluechtlinge-ukraine-105.html
[131] https://www.tagesschau.de/newsticker/liveblog-ukraine-krieg-donnerstag-101.html
[132] https://www.tagesschau.de/ausland/ukraine-polen-fluechtlinge-101.html
[133] https://www.spiegel.de/ausland/russland-so-wurde-wladimir-putin-wie-er-ist-a-c77ae46d-4be1-4413-9dab-94b2500726ea
[134] https://nsn.fm/hots/hots-putin-rasskazal-o-zagnannoy-v-ugol-kryse
[135] https://www.nzz.ch/international/ukraine-krieg-putin-verspielt-russlands-zukunft-ld.1671913
[136] https://www.bild.de/unterhaltung/leute/leute/us-praesident-joe-biden-droht-reichen-russen-wir-holen-uns-eure-yachten-und-priv-79332752.bild.html
[137] https://www.bz-berlin.de/welt/russischer-geschaeftsmann-setzt-1-million-dollar-kopfgeld-auf-putin-aus
[138] https://www.cnbctv18.com/world/russia-ukraine-war-kyiv-moscow-trade-blame-over-failed-evacuation-as-assault-grinds-on-12714982.htm
[139] https://de.statista.com/statistik/daten/studie/15722/umfrage/export-von-guetern-aus-china/
[140] https://de.statista.com/statistik/daten/studie/37013/umfrage/ranking-der-top-20-exportlaender-weltweit/

[141] https://de.statista.com/statistik/daten/studie/219312/umfrage/waehrungsreserven-von-china/
[142] https://www.treasury.gov/resource-center/data-chart-center/IR-Position/Pages/11182016.aspx
[143] https://www.tagesschau.de/ausland/asien/volkskongress-china-131.html
[144] https://www.census.gov/foreign-trade/balance/c5700.html
[145] https://www.deutschlandfunk.de/memorandum-portugal-wird-teil-chinas-neuer-seidenstrasse.795.de.html
[146] https://www.zeit.de/wirtschaft/2018-04/neue-seidenstrasse-china-griechenland-europa-containerhafen-piraeus
[147] https://www.zeit.de/2017/39/china-investitionen-einfluss-europa
[148] https://www.welt.de/wirtschaft/article190779455/Neue-Seidenstrasse-Italien-schert-aus-und-einigt-sich-mit-China.html
[149] https://www.nzz.ch/schweiz/seidenstrasse-bundesrat-wollte-vereinbarung-zu-menschenrechten-ld.1479438
[150] https://www.handelsblatt.com/politik/international/welthandel-chinas-marsch-nach-westen-wie-gefaehrlich-die-neue-seidenstrasse-wirklich-ist/24155726.html
[151] https://www.tagesspiegel.de/politik/ein-massiver-politischer-erfolg-fuer-china-was-das-asiatische-freihandelsabkommen-fuer-eu-und-usa-bedeutet/26629946.html
[152] https://www.wirtschaftsdienst.eu/inhalt/jahr/2019/heft/8/beitrag/handelsbilanz-streit-zwischen-den-usa-und-china.html
[153] https://www.heise.de/tp/news/China-Eskalation-im-Handelskrieg-mit-den-USA-4110409.html
[154] https://www.bloomberg.com/features/2020-future-after-coronavirus/
[155] https://www.spiegel.de/politik/ausland/uno-antonio-guterres-warnt-vor-kaltem-krieg-zwischen-den-usa-und-china-a-3b59429b-56d5-4a3a-9ae8-05f4a1d77968
[156] https://www.handelsblatt.com/politik/international/handelsstreit-trump-erwaegt-angeblich-chinesische-firmen-von-us-boersen-auszuschliessen/25065040.html
[157] https://www.faz.net/aktuell/wirtschaft/digitec/apple-feiert-ein-rekordquartal-dank-des-iphone-17457684.html
[158] https://www.derbund.ch/die-geschaefte-von-apple-und-alphabet-boomen-752866100118
[159] https://www.nytimes.com/2021/05/17/technology/apple-china-censorship-data.html
[160] https://www.wiwo.de/my/unternehmen/dienstleister/kuscht-biontech-vor-peking-die-spektakulaersten-kniefaelle-vor-china-/27237110.html?ticket=ST-518618-QEtra-oVEoVC4WFrrfa6v-ap6
[161] https://www.freiheit.org/de/suedost-und-ostasien/das-biontech-drama-taiwan
[162] https://www.heise.de/news/LoongArch-China-hat-eigenen-CPU-Befehlssatz-fertig-entwickelt-6019624.html
[163] https://www.tagesschau.de/ausland/asien/volkskongress-china-131.html
[164] https://www.btc-echo.de/weltpremiere-china-startet-digitales-zentralbanken-geld-cbdc/
[165] https://www.btc-echo.de/weltpremiere-china-startet-digitales-zentralbanken-geld-cbdc/
[166] Der Spiegel 27/2019

[167] https://www.zeit.de/politik/ausland/2018-08/idlib-baschar-al-assad-syrien-chemie-waffen-westmaechte-warnung
[168] https://www.heise.de/tp/features/Fast-die-Haelfte-der-US-Soldaten-erwartet-demnaechst-einen-groesseren-Krieg-4195444.html
[169] https://www.spiegel.de/ausland/folge-von-cyberangriff-us-praesident-joe-biden-warnt-vor-echtem-krieg-a-66f2acff-7baa-4af5-85b4-0a4c8d30de6b
[170] https://www.spiegel.de/politik/ausland/donald-trump-und-seine-militaerstrategie-vorsprung-des-us-militaers-schrumpft-a-1238449.html
[171] https://www.spiegel.de/politik/ausland/ex-general-richard-barrons-ueber-den-krieg-der-zukunft-kampfroboter-bekommen-keine-pension-a-058c61c5-e4c2-4845-9d0e-33f3a7a3e4cc
[172] https://www.n-tv.de/politik/Ruestungswettlauf-ist-in-vollem-Gange-article20690888.html
[173] https://www.bpb.de/apuz/26873/funktionen-militaerischer-konfliktregelung-durch-die-nato?p=all
[174] https://www.msn.com/en-gb/news/uknews/defence-secretary-ben-wallace-some-people-will-be-left-behind-in-afghanistan/ar-AANAP2K
[175] http://www.balladen.de/web/sites/balladen_gedichte/autoren.php?b05=8&b16=709
[176] https://www.msn.com/en-gb/news/uknews/defence-secretary-ben-wallace-some-people-will-be-left-behind-in-afghanistan/ar-AANAP2K
[177] https://www.sigar.mil/pdf/lessonslearned/SIGAR-21-46-LL.pdf
[178] https://www.t-online.de/nachrichten/ausland/krisen/id_90622056/taliban-marsch-auf-kabul-der-fall-afghanistan-zeigt-die-schwaeche-des-westens-.html
[179] https://www.heise.de/tp/features/Anhaltender-Krieg-in-Afghanistan-verursacht-schwere-Umweltschaeden-3414967.html
[180] Joseph J. Collins: Understanding War in Afghanistan. National Defense University Press, Washington, D.C. 2011. ISBN 978-1-78039-924-9
[181] https://de.wikipedia.org/wiki/Sowjetische_Intervention_in_Afghanistan#cite_note-18
[182] https://www.tagesschau.de/ausland/asien/afghanistan-taliban-behoerden-101.html
[183] https://www.washingtonexaminer.com/news/zawahiri-video-al-qaeda-alive-well-taliban-takeover
[184] https://www.n-tv.de/politik/05-35-Tschechiens-Praesident-warnt-vor-Terrorbasis--article22743909.html
[185] https://www.tagesschau.de/ausland/moskau-afghanistan-101.html
[186] https://www.spiegel.de/ausland/afghanistan-russland-warnt-die-usa-vor-truppenstationierung-in-zentralasien-a-ca0af8e7-30c3-4be6-a65d-0a5bca9d5973#ref=rss
[187] https://www.tagesschau.de/ausland/china-afghanistan-105.html
[188] https://www.handelsblatt.com/politik/international/geopolitics-das-grosse-wettrennen-um-afghanistans-rohstoffe-hat-begonnen/27521122.html
[189] https://www.tagesschau.de/wirtschaft/weltwirtschaft/afghanistan-rohstoffe-bodenschaetze-china-101.html
[190] https://www.dw.com/de/afghanistan-der-billionenschatz-der-taliban/a-58897871

[191] https://www.handelsblatt.com/politik/international/verteidigungsunion-der-weg-zur-eu-armee-ist-steinig-kommt-stattdessen-die-armee-der-willigen/23790020.html?ticket=ST-2485103-rSTFNhtgUhR1DroqifLk-ap4

[192] https://www.handelsblatt.com/politik/international/reaktion-auf-russland-nato-schliesst-diskussion-ueber-atomare-nachruestung-nicht-mehr-aus/23827392.html

[193] https://www.bmvg.de/de/themen/dossiers/europaeische-sicherheit-und-verteidigung/pesco

[194] https://www.wienerzeitung.at/nachrichten/politik/europa/963138-Hintergrund-Die-Militaerkooperation-PESCO.html

[195] https://www.tagesschau.de/ausland/europa/weber-cyberarmee-101.html

[196] https://www.nordbayern.de/region/bomber-uber-der-region-aufgetaucht-was-trieb-die-b-52-in-grafenwohr-1.11898006

[197] https://www.zeit.de/politik/ausland/2019-04/sipri-bericht-weltweite-militaerausgaben-neuer-hoechststand

[198] https://www.dw.com/de/studie-militärausgaben-steigen-weltweit/a-52382220

[199] https://de.statista.com/statistik/daten/studie/157935/umfrage/laender-mit-den-hoechsten-militaerausgaben/

[200] https://www.spiegel.de/politik/ausland/atomwaffen-sipri-forscher-warnen-vor-neuem-wettruesten-a-53280e50-8488-480b-a723-6509022097a6

[201] https://www.welt.de/politik/ausland/plus220132704/Kampfmaschinen-Flash-War-nennen-Experten-dieses-Szenario.html?

[202] https://www.auswaertiges-amt.de/de/aussenpolitik/themen/abruestung-ruestungskontrolle/autonome-waffen/2241938

[203] https://www.swissinfo.ch/ger/politik/autonome-waffensysteme_was-bringen-uno-gespraeche-ueber-killerroboter-/4403213

[204] 75 Jahre UNO – Macht und Ohnmacht der Vereinten Nationen, Andreas Dripke, Hang Nguyen, DC Publishing, ISBN 978-3-947818-07-5

[205] https://www.zeit.de/gesellschaft/zeitgeschehen/2020-12/chang-e-5-china-mond-mission-flagge-mond

[206] https://www.spiegel.de/ausland/folge-von-cyberangriff-us-praesident-joe-biden-warnt-vor-echtem-krieg-a-66f2acff-7baa-4af5-85b4-0a4c8d30de6b

[207] Stasi 2.0 – Wie wir durch den staatlich-industriellen Digitalkomplex zu gläsernen Bürgern werden und was das für unsere Zukunft bedeutet, Andreas Dripke, Markus Miksch, ISBN 978-3-947818-05-1

[208] https://www.msn.com/de-de/nachrichten/finance-top-stories/studie-schäden-durch-cyberkriminalität-übersteigen-eine-billion-dollar/ar-BB1bl2w8

[209] https://www.darkreading.com/operational-security/microsofts-brad-smith-2017-was-a-cybersecurity-wake-up-call/a/d-id/742337

[210] https://www.spiegel.de/politik/ausland/coronavirus-impfstoff-cyberangriff-auf-impfstoff-dokumente-von-biontech-a-2d1e2574-8ee6-4a52-999a-34bc0dacef7e

[211] Stockholm International Peace Research Institute SIPRI Yearbook 2018, Oxford University Press, ISBN 978-0-19-882155-7

[212] https://www.heise.de/tp/features/Gefahr-eines-Krieges-mit-Russland-und-China-4221421.html

[213] https://www.washingtonpost.com/news/josh-rogin/wp/2018/11/13/pence-its-up-to-china-to-avoid-a-cold-war/

[214] https://www.stern.de/politik/ausland/russland--wladimir-putin-warnt-vor-atomkrieg-und-gibt-usa-die-schuld-8500618.html

[215] http://bos.sagepub.com/content/62/4/64

[216] https://www.deutschlandfunk.de/am-rande-der-katastrophe.871.de.html?dram:article_id=126035

[217] https://www.spiegel.de/spiegel/print/d-15433373.html

[218] https://portal.dnb.de/opac.htm?method=simpleSearch&query=4136402-8

[219] Henry A. Kissinger: *Memoiren 1973-1974*, Band 2, Munich 1982, ISBN 3-570-00710-3

[220] https://www.zeit.de/politik/ausland/2018-10/inf-vertrag-usa-donald-trump-russland-abruestungsvereinbarung-kuendigen

[221] https://de.nachrichten.yahoo.com/russland-legt-resolutionsentwurf-inf-abrüstungsabkommen-005537819.html

[222] https://www.heise.de/tp/features/Chinas-Verteidigungsstrategie-ist-gegen-die-USA-ausgerichtet-4489383.html

[223] https://www.nytimes.com/2021/07/26/us/politics/china-nuclear-weapons.html

[224] https://www.washingtonpost.com/national-security/china-nuclear-missile-silos/2021/06/30/0fa8debc-d9c2-11eb-bb9e-70fda8c37057_story.html

[225] https://www.spiegel.de/ausland/china-so-feiert-das-land-den-100-jahrestag-der-kommunistischen-partei-a-36ca1892-c846-4145-9c89-26777393a216

[226] https://www.spiegel.de/politik/ausland/nordkorea-besitzt-wahrscheinlich-atomwaffen-in-sprengkopfgroesse-uno-bericht-a-f580d767-f9f3-49a6-ada3-658c11ac481d

[227] https://www.iaea.org/about/statute#A1.2

[228] https://www.t-online.de/nachrichten/ausland/usa/id_45962710/al-baradei-geht-mit-bush-regierung-hart-ins-gericht-.html

[229] https://www.sueddeutsche.de/politik/irak-bushs-kriegsschuld-1.3068877

[230] https://www.atomwaffena-z.info/heute/die-atomwaffenfreie-welt

[231] https://www.spiegel.de/wirtschaft/unternehmen/iran-us-botschafter-richard-grenell-lobt-rueckzug-deutscher-firmen-a-1239755.html

[232] https://www.dailymail.co.uk/news/article-10024535/China-prepared-strike-using-nukes-diplomat-says.html

[233] https://www.dailymail.co.uk/news/article-10024535/China-prepared-strike-using-nukes-diplomat-says.html

CPSIA information can be obtained
at www.ICGtesting.com
Printed in the USA
LVHW081153200422
716646LV00014B/516

9 783986 740221